This book is due for return on or before the last date shown below.

Emile Gallé

Emile Gallé

TIM NEWARK

THE
APPLE
PRESS

For my mother, who enjoys the Musée d'Orsay

A QUINTET BOOK

Published by The Apple Press
6 Blundell Street
London, N7 9BH

ISBN 1-85076-180-9

This book was designed and produced by
Quintet Publishing Limited
6 Blundell Street
London N7 9BH

Creative Director: Peter Bridgewater
Art Director: Ian Hunt
Designer: Nicki Simmonds
Project Editor: Judith Simons
Editor: Henrietta Wilkinson
Illustrator: Lorraine Harrison

Typeset in Great Britain by
Central Southern Typesetters, Eastbourne
Manufactured in Hong Kong by
Regent Publishing Services Limited
Printed in Hong Kong by
Leefung-Asco Printers Limited

CONTENTS

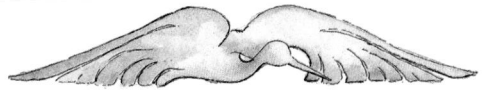

C H A P T E R   O N E
PARIS 1900

ABOVE The Palace of Electricity at the Paris Universal Exhibition of 1900. From a painting by Edward Thiel, reproduced in a catalogue of the exhibition.

THE EXPOSITION UNIVERSELLE held in Paris in 1900 was billed as the 'Exhibition of the Century', with 120 million francs spent on it and over 40 million visitors in six months. Summing up the grandest achievements in art and science of the 19th century, it also heralded a new century of even greater wonders, symbolized by the Palace of Electricity, a mighty power-station which cast a halo of artificial light over Paris.

Every western, or westernized, country of the world was represented by its own pavilion, built along the Left Bank of the Seine. Their colonies, from Africa to Asia, were represented by life-size reconstructions of native villages and Oriental temples.

'Behold this spectacle,' wrote Anatole France, describing the panorama of the exhibition. 'Look: domes, minarets, steeples, towers, pediments, roofs of thatch, of glass, of tiles, of coloured earthenware, of wood and animal hides, Italian terraces and Moorish terraces, palaces, temples, pagodas, kiosks, huts, cabins, tents, water-towers, contrasts and harmonies of all kinds of human habitation, the fever of work, the wonderful labour of industry, the enormous amusement of the genius of man, who has planted here the arts and crafts of the universe.'

Seen by most visitors as simply a giant fun-fair, it was regarded with greater seriousness by the leading exhibiting nations. There were some 76,000 exhibitors and over half of these came from abroad. For them, the Exposition Universelle was a cultural Olympics in which the major powers competed for the attention and praise of the world.

In the main events, Great Britain and America fared badly. The British pavilion was a mock-Elizabethan mansion designed by Edwin Lutyens, but inside the art and furniture was distinctly disappointing. Any anonymous reviewer was less polite: 'The English, puffed up with pride, are afraid that not many people will visit their pavilion, which is like a middle-class house in Newhaven. They have put an attendant in front of the closed door. He says the door will shortly be opened and the crowd gathers, there being enough naïve people to queue. This trick is often used by dentists. The Americans did little better: 'In the United States pavilion,' commented the same reviewer, 'there is nothing. Some tables, chairs, newspapers, letter-boxes, and that's all. Obviously, these people don't waste their time on trivialities. One well-equipped post-office and you have seen America.'

Overall, it was the European continental exhibitors who were the winners. It was they, and France in particular, who understood the new art and design of 1900. Throughout the French pavilions and galleries, Art Nouveau was the energy of the exhibition, and chief among her artistic Olympians was Emile Gallé (1846–1904).

Gallé had been preparing for this exhibition for several years. He usually showed his glassware and furniture annually at the Salon du Champ-de-Mars in Paris, but for the previous couple of years he held back his finest works. He wanted to amaze his audience. Just as the Exposition Universelle was to be a review of 19th-century design as a whole so Gallé intended his display to be a summing up of his personal aims and achievements. Envelopes in pastel shades stamped with flower insignia enclosed a catalogue listing his exhibits and maps of where to see them. They were sent to all his friends and patrons. What they saw was a surprise even to his closest colleagues.

In one pavilion, Gallé had a complete glass furnace built. Craftsmen demonstrated the blowing of glass, the ground scattered with fragments of pieces that had cracked in the process, showing the intense labour and degree of perfection needed to produce an individual vase. Above the mouth of the furnace, he placed a suitably dramatic maxim: 'But if men should be wicked, perverters of truth and justice, come to

Italien.   Türkei.   Ver. Staaten von Nord-Amerika.   Österreich

Weltausstellung zu Paris: Die Repräsentations-Gebäud

Nach einem Aquar

ABOVE General view of the national pavilions at the Paris Universal Exhibition. From left to right are the pavilions of Italy, Turkey, the United States of America, Austria, Bosnia, Hungary, Britain, Belgium, Germany, Spain and Sweden. Taken from a painting by Georges Scott.

Ungarn. England. Belgien. Deutschland. Spanien. Schweden.   Pavillon der Stadt Paris.

nden Staaten am Ufer der Seine (Quai d'Orsay).

s Scott.

ABOVE Visitors to the Paris Universal Exhibition being pushed in wheelchairs to pavilions situated far apart.

OPPOSITE *L'Orchidée* (*The Orchid*) vase, 1900, made of applied and engraved glass.

my help you demons of fire. Let vases break and the furnaces crumble so that all men learn to be just' – the blowing of glass required moral virtue, strictly in accord with his Protestant faith. Around the furnace stood vases ancient and modern, showing just how Gallé and his factory at Nancy stood at the very summit of contemporary glassware.

Gallé displayed objects from every stage of his career so connoisseurs could trace the development of his style, but for the general viewer it was his latest work that possessed the greatest excitement. His experiments with chemical combinations produced colours of remarkable fire, deep glowing shades, copying and surpassing the natural lustre of plants and animals. His artistry took him into the realm of glass sculpture as he applied forms of molten glass to his vases, modelling them while still soft into beautifully detailed flowers. *L'Orchidée* (The Orchid) was a triumph of this technique, attaching a delicately folded pink orchid to its green and blue base. *Le Lys* (The Lily) had its translucent white petals sensuously embracing the flesh pink vase, while *Les Têtards* (Tadpoles) was a foray into natural history with larvae swimming up sides streaked with liquid blues.

Gallé's furniture for the exhibition was no less innovative. The heavy Rococo decoration of his early woodwork was replaced by light, elegant chairs and tables with sinuous lines based on plant stems. The openwork back of a sofa bore carved heads of wheat, while *Commode à l'Ipomea*, carved in ash and walnut, was inlaid with a maxim close to his heart: 'Travail est joie chez Gallé' (Work is joy for Gallé). His love of exotic woods was indulged in a firescreen carved in ash, its serpentine spray of leaves inlaid in a mosaic of oak, zebrawood, sabicu, amboyna and walnut. *La Forêt Lorraine* was a magical writing desk conjuring up images of Gallé's childhood in the forests of Lorraine. It contained a reference to a poem by Baudelaire, inscribed in fruitwood, which invited the writer at the desk to explore a world of the imagination.

Many of these items were exhibited in showcases, but in the pavilion of the Union Centrale des Arts Décoratifs, whole rooms were created as settings for the perfect interiors, combining all the furnishings of the most modern craftsmen and artists. Fortunately, one of the rooms was bought by the Musée des Arts Décoratifs in Paris and can be seen today reconstructed with all its original detail, including vases by Gallé. The room was designed by Georges Hoentschel, a potter and architect, who applied nature directly to his decoration. Wooden panels and columns were carved like trees; a piano bore a wood inlay landscape with fluttering doves; in glass cases against the wall stood jewellery by René Lalique; and on a table by Hector Guimard was a strange, sumptuous vase by Gallé, called *Thistles*.

ABOVE *Rose de France* vase, c.1900, made of applied glass.

OPPOSITE Room designed by George Hoendschel for the Paris Universal Exhibition, and now preserved in the Musée des Arts Décoratifs, Paris.

THISTLES AND SYMBOLISM

This vase acted as a perfect symbol for many of Gallé's passions throughout his life. The very shape of the vase – and the bubbling glass at the bottom – represented the cone and immature leaves of an unopened thistle, but on its side is painted a mature thistle with its purple cotton top. Decoration and form are thus combined to show two different stages in the development of the one flower, a decorative vision of nature which Gallé applied throughout his work, always seeking the botanical truth behind his decoration and yet maintaining its artistic beauty.

On top of this, the thistle was a political symbol. 'We are fully aware that the eloquence of a flower', he wrote, 'often surpasses the authority of the human figure in the intensity of its suggestive power. We know that the expression in our own heraldic thistle, for instance, relates to a defiant gesture.' The thistle was the symbol of the province of Lorraine and its capital, Nancy, where Gallé lived and worked. Ever since the region had been annexed by the Germans in the Franco-Prussian War, Gallé had used the symbol of the thistle as a sign of continued protest at the invasion of his homeland. He fully intended his glasswork and furniture to be more than just bourgeois decoration: it was art, full of profound statements on nature, politics and history. And it was this many-layered aspect of his work that excited intellectuals of the day, ensuring that his display at the Exposition Universelle was a critical, as well as financial, success.

Thistles vase, 1900, exhibited at the Paris Universal Exhibition. Mould blown and with marquetry inlays, it stands 17in/44cm high.

Gallé's career had peaked. At the age of 54, he was widely regarded as one of the leading artists of France. He had been elected to the Légion d'Honneur and went on to represent France at the Turin Exhibition of 1902. He had already won gold medals for his work at the 1889 Paris Exposition Universelle and the Chicago Exposition of 1893. His work was commissioned by governments, by the City of Paris, the Russian Royal Family and the Institute of Louis Pasteur. His work was sought after by writers such as Marcel Proust and noted collectors of modern art, including Roger Marx, editor of the *Gazette des Beaux-Arts*, and Edouard Hannon, an industrialist with an Art Nouveau house in Brussels. Commercially, Gallé's factory in Nancy produced glassware and furniture that was sold throughout Europe and North America, with shops in Paris, London and Frankfurt.

After the Exposition Universelle, he could easily have stayed on in Paris, mixing with the fashion-leaders of French society to which the Symbolist poet and aesthete, Count Robert de Montesquiou-Fezensac (1855–1921), had introduced him. Although it was clear he enjoyed the attention and company of these stimulating people, he also appears to have been awkward among them, allowing his enthusiasm to bubble over, rather than maintain 'artistic aloofness'. Instead, he was happy to leave the adulation for a prompt return to Nancy. It was there that he had received his education in nature and the practicalities of glass craftsmanship, and it was there that he dreamed his most fantastic ideas. Nancy was the home of Gallé's genius.

OPPOSITE Dragonfly coupe, 1904, of blown glass, marquetry with metallic foil inclusions and patination, then cut and engraved.

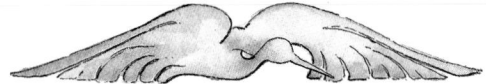

CHAPTER TWO

GROWING UP

ABOVE Medieval-style *verrerie
parlante*, 1884–1900, inscribed
*'La Ballade des Dames du Temps
Jadis'* – after a poem by François
Villon.

CHARLES GALLÉ, EMILE GALLÉ'S FATHER, arrived in Nancy in 1844. The capital city of Lorraine in north east France had a reputation in the 18th century for elegance and culture. The exiled king of Poland, Duke Stanislas Leczinsky, had made his home there, and much of the Rococo ornament on its buildings reflected a general rise in its prosperity. Nancy also had a history of glassmaking, stemming from the Middle Ages, and when Charles Gallé arrived he was attracted by the possibilities of this business. Equipped only with the skills of a draughtsman and a nose for enterprise, his first break came with his marriage to Mademoiselle Reinemer. The daughter of a mirror manufacturer, Charles saw ample opportunity for expansion in her family business and added table glassware to their manufacturing. Taking his inspiration from the then still fashionable Rococo motifs all around Nancy, he produced a series of glassworks with florid shapes and decoration. His enamelling technique for colouring the glass was crude, but it proved immensely popular and the greatest honour came when the Emperor of France included Gallé glass among his tableware at his houses in Biarritz, Saint Cloud, and Compiègne.

Ever restless for more opportunities, Charles Gallé bought up a series of old moulds from a local pottery, and with new heraldic designs painted on them, he created a second series of tableware as popular as the first. It was into this success of commerce and craft that Emile Gallé was born in 1846. Careful not to pull his son too early into the family business, Charles gave Emile a solid Protestant education. He shone in philosophy, Latin and French literature, winning several school prizes, and also studied the natural sciences under Professor DA Godron, author of an important French book on flowers. In later years, Emile was to complain that his formal education had been too academic and had not prepared him for the practicalities of his family craft, but this was harsh and unjust criticism. His studies gave him a great love and knowledge of both literature and science which was to enrich his work and set it apart from any previous glassworker's.

Allowed four years of further education, Emile travelled to Germany where he managed to spend time in the Saar glassworks of Burgun, Schwerer & Co, learning the chemistry and technology of glassmaking. By this stage, he was already contributing designs to his

LEFT Portrait of Emile Gallé working in his studio, 1892, by Victor Prouvé, his long time friend and business partner.

father's ceramic tableware and had established a firm friendship with
Victor Prouvé (1858–1943), the son of one of his father's craftsmen.
Together, they began to experiment with the design and manufacture
of glass, learning much from both their fathers. Victor Prouvé senior
was responsible for creating the most popular pottery figures at that
time – a heraldic lion grasping a tower and painted in vivid blue and
gold. Its medieval and Rococo elements excited Gallé's imagination,
but this happy evolution was interrupted by the outbreak of war in
1870.

Prussia, under the confident command of Bismarck, invaded
Lorraine and pushed towards Paris, inflicting humiliating defeats on
the French. Emile enlisted as a volunteer infantryman of the line. He
saw little action and by the following year the war was over, with
Prussia demanding, and receiving, the provinces of Alsace and Lorraine.
With the German frontier now only a few miles from Nancy, Emile
Gallé never forgot or forgave this violation of his homeland. Demobi-
lized, he joined his father on a trip to London to organize an exhibition
of French art, and used much of the time to study designs at the

South Kensington Museum (now the Victoria and Albert Museum) and plants at Kew Gardens.

Returning to France, Gallé visited Paris before travelling to Italy and Switzerland. He was absorbing ideas by the dozen, admiring the work of past ages and cultures – the bold forms of medieval glass, the intricate patterns of Islamic pottery. But the style with which he felt the greatest sympathy was that of French Rococo. By then over-elaborated, caricatured and hackneyed, it nevertheless possessed a fluidity of line and asymmetry that reflected the vigour of natural design; that naturalness was closer to Gallé's interests than anything else he had seen. In the great museums of Europe, he discovered the roots of Rococo and saw at first hand the brilliance of the craftsmen who initiated the style in the early 18th century.

At the heart of the Rococo was the desire to explore and imitate the forms of nature. By combining the flowing asymmetric rock of a grotto with the curving ribs of a shell and the swirling lines of leaves and stems, they invented a style that was admirably suited to the construction of furniture and *objets d'art*. Gallé had spent his childhood admiring the random forms of nature and wondering how to adapt them to his own craft, and in the Rococo he found both inspiration and education. The greatest exponent of the early Rococo was undoubtedly Juste-Aurèle Meissonnier (1695–1750); his exquisitely rendered gold- and silverware would undoubtedly have influenced the young Gallé.

A silver tureen designed by Meissonnier between 1734 and 1740 epitomizes his style, and is the most explicit in its references to nature. A shell-shaped tureen, it rested upon legs of cast and chased bunches of celery, cabbage leaves, onion and a carrot. The cover, also shell-shaped and ribbed, was decorated with a duck, crab, fish, oyster and barnacles, all in silver and all meticulously modelled, right down to the ridges on the shells of the crabs and barnacles – so much so, in fact, that some art historians claimed they were actually cast from real shellfish. This remarkable tureen was designed to hold *oglio*, a stew of mixed meats popular in the 18th century, so in effect Meissonnier had turned the contents of the tureen inside out. This was design at its wittiest and most ingenious, and must have struck a chord with Gallé for he went on to create glassware that took both plant and animal forms literally to create shapes of equal exuberance.

In 1873, Gallé's father built a grand family house in Nancy in solid bourgeois style. Nicknamed *La Garenne* (the rabbit warren), it was a symbol of his success and of his pride in his achievement; a family house for a family business. It was also a home where he could begin to sit back and enjoy overseeing his son take charge. He provided him

LEFT Enamelled glass bottle and liqueur set, 1890s, decorated with insects, thistles and the Cross of Lorraine.

ABOVE Enamelled glass bowl, 1890s, decorated with sprays of catkins and an 18th-century style cartouche.

OPPOSITE Syrian-style vase, *c.*1880, showing Gallé's early eclectic use of Arabic pattern.

with a workshop and studio in the house, but Emile wanted more. He convinced his father to bring all their factories and workshops from neighbouring regions together and concentrate them in Nancy. A year later, Gallé senior could see his son was in control and retired completely. The year after that, Emile married Henriette Grimm, the daughter of a local Protestant pastor. She was also the inheritor of a shop selling mirrors, but Emile had no use for the shop and sold it immediately. His sights were set on more ambitious projects.

By 1878, Emile Gallé had sent his first collection of glassware to the Decorative Arts exhibition in Paris. He had also expanded the family glassworks, building new furnaces and workshops only a few hundred yards from *La Garenne*. During the 1870s and 1880s he experimented with different styles on the way to establishing his own, and was strongly aware of the prevailing fashion for medievalism. Medieval Syrian and Venetian glass provided him with a starting point for learning the application of enamels. He added more adventurous shades to their crude primary colours until he had a palette including pinks and violets, half-shades and pastels. He made the enamel translucent so it absorbed light, giving it a livelier lustre. And from the European literature of legends, he took the decorative themes of heraldic motifs and the imagery of knights and their ladies.

Japanese art provided Gallé with similar inspiration, encouraging him to push out the bounds of contemporary glass in shape and content. He learnt the expressive power of the line, and how to abstract a flower and yet still retain its essence. A specific explanation for this

impact on his work was provided by the presence of a Japanese student in Nancy. In 1885, Tokouso Takashima came to study botany at the Ecole Forestier and he quickly became friends with Gallé and the other leading artists of Nancy – so much so that a critic wrote after Gallé's 1889 Paris show: 'Let us bless the whims of fate which caused a Japanese to be born in Nancy.' The writer is, of course, referring to Gallé and his strongly Oriental work of that year, including a collection of glassware incorporating Chinese motifs and a new sealing-wax red enamel resembling lacquer. He even adopted a Japanese-style signature. But all this was simply a sense of fun, a nod towards fashion and the copying of other styles to strengthen his own.

What Gallé most responded to in Japanese art was its reverence for natural forms, particularly flowers. This brought him back full circle to the most profound pleasure of his life. From early childhood he had adored summer evenings rambling through the countryside around Nancy, spotting wild flowers, sketching their colours and shapes. This graduated into a scientific study of botany and now, strolling through the overgrown garden around his family home, he had at last the confidence in his own skills to apply this passion directly to glass. It was the beginning of his greatest achievement.

ABOVE Enamelled glass dish, 1890s, with a Japanese-style decoration of herons and clouds.

OPPOSITE *Vase à la Carpe*, 1876, a magnificent example of oriental influences on Gallé's work.

C H A P T E R   T H R E E
NATURE

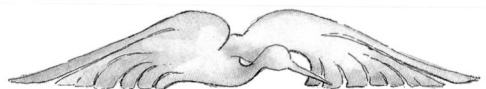

ABOVE Dragonfly table, *c.*1900, with marquetry, standing 29½in/ 75cm high.

Gallé's appreciation of nature was ecstatic, verging on the religious. In an essay on the philosophy behind his work, he wrote that beauty was truth and that truth lay in nature. He believed that our very existence depended on the abundance of plants. Referring to a contemporary biologist, he said: 'It was Moleschott who stated that plants, in their turn, make air. He said it is by their grace that we live on the earth, that they are our roots, that we are able to think because they vegetate, that virgin forests transform themselves little by little into fruits of the field and new men, that each day salutes a new world, that in this way at each sunrise everything is eternally new.' Gallé then applied this vision to himself. 'As I sit at my *table potagère*, beneath a cluster of strawberries, looking towards a stream springing from the veins of the wood, I simply transcribe my feeling of gratitude to the plants, those nourishers of our bodies and our arts, to our common fatherland – the ancient forest whose edge we cultivate.' It is a surprisingly relevant image to the late 20th-century age of Gaia, the new biology in which the world is viewed as one living organism, dependent on each aspect of its nature for survival, but giving special value to the plant world.

In the early 19th century, nature was valued for its reflection of God. Like many Christian natural historians of the time, John Lindley, Professor of Botany at University College, London, wrote: 'The power and wisdom of the Deity are proclaimed by no part of Creation in more impressive language than by the humblest weed that we tread beneath our feet.' John Ruskin, the English art critic, took up this concept of God in nature and based his aesthetic appreciation upon it. He insisted that curved lines were more beautiful than straight lines. Shades of colour were more beautiful than plane surfaces. Not just because that was the way things were in nature, but because the multitude of shades and degrees of curve expressed the infinity of God – 'a clear infinity, the darkness of the pure unsearchable sea'.

As the century progressed, Ruskin's idea of art based on nature being good because it spoke of God lost its power. Science proved that nature was not necessarily beneficient and that it existed separately from God. But the desire among artists and intellectuals for a closer relationship with nature was not abandoned. Critics agreed that curves were more pleasing than lines because they imitated the subtleties of

ABOVE Floral vases, *c.*1900, with applied glass and *marqueterie de verre.*

nature. Christopher Dresser (1834–1904), the multi-talented Briton, was trained as a botanist before deciding in 1860 to become an industrial designer. He believed nature served as an excellent model for construction, and of one of his designs, he wrote: 'I have sought to embody chiefly the one idea of power energy, force or vigour, as a dominant idea; and in order to do this, I have employed such lines as we see in the bursting buds of spring, when the energy of growth is at its maximum, and especially such as are to be seen in the spring growth of a luxuriant tropical vegetation.' Such ideas formed the aesthetics behind Art Nouveau, in which the shape and decoration of furniture could be derived directly from organic forms.

In Nancy, Gallé hung the motto: 'Our roots are in the depth of the woods – on the banks of streams, among the mosses' above the door of his studio. After his death, his wife wrote: 'If Emile Gallé has renewed the decorative arts, it is from having studied plants, trees, flowers, both as an artist and scholar.' Gallé credited this passion to his upbringing. 'Luckily, the love of the flower reigned in my family,' he recorded, 'it

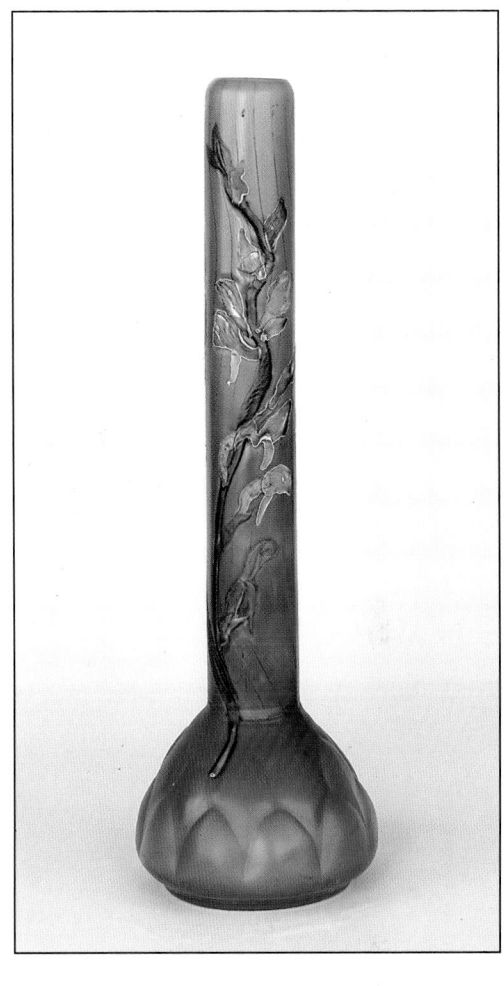

was a hereditary passion. It was salvation. I knew something of the natural sciences. I followed the botany of Godron, author of *Flores de Lorraine et de France*. My father, on his crystal glass, his porcelain, had made studies of the fields, reproducing Graminacea and blooming grasses.'

But Gallé's decorative principles were wholly founded on a close study of nature and his forms are more naturalistic than those of the majority of his contemporaries. The flowers and plants on his vases retained their illusionistic effect without becoming two-dimensional patterns. Other artists in Nancy, such as Jean-Auguste Dampt, also claimed this inspiration, exclaiming 'Always, always art is the essence of Nature refined, purified and synthesized, through the medium of an artist's temperament which should not copy it, but transform and stylize it.' But Gallé's would not be stylized to the point of becoming a mere pattern, empty of life. He would not smooth or reduce its vigour. If nature was awkward, he would design a vase or table to fit the form of the chosen plant. Unlike his Art Nouveau contemporaries, nature was more than just a ready to hand model book. With spiritual outlook closer to Ruskin and the natural theologians earlier in the century, Gallé believed in the mystical qualities of plants and flowers. His pro-

OPPOSITE A pair of cameo vases, *c.*1900, 20in/51cm high.

ABOVE LEFT *Rose de France* vase, *c.*1900, made of applied glass.

ABOVE RIGHT Vase, *c.*1900, made of *marqueterie de verre*, and standing 20in/51cm high.

RIGHT *Rose de France* vase of applied glass, 7½in/19cm high.

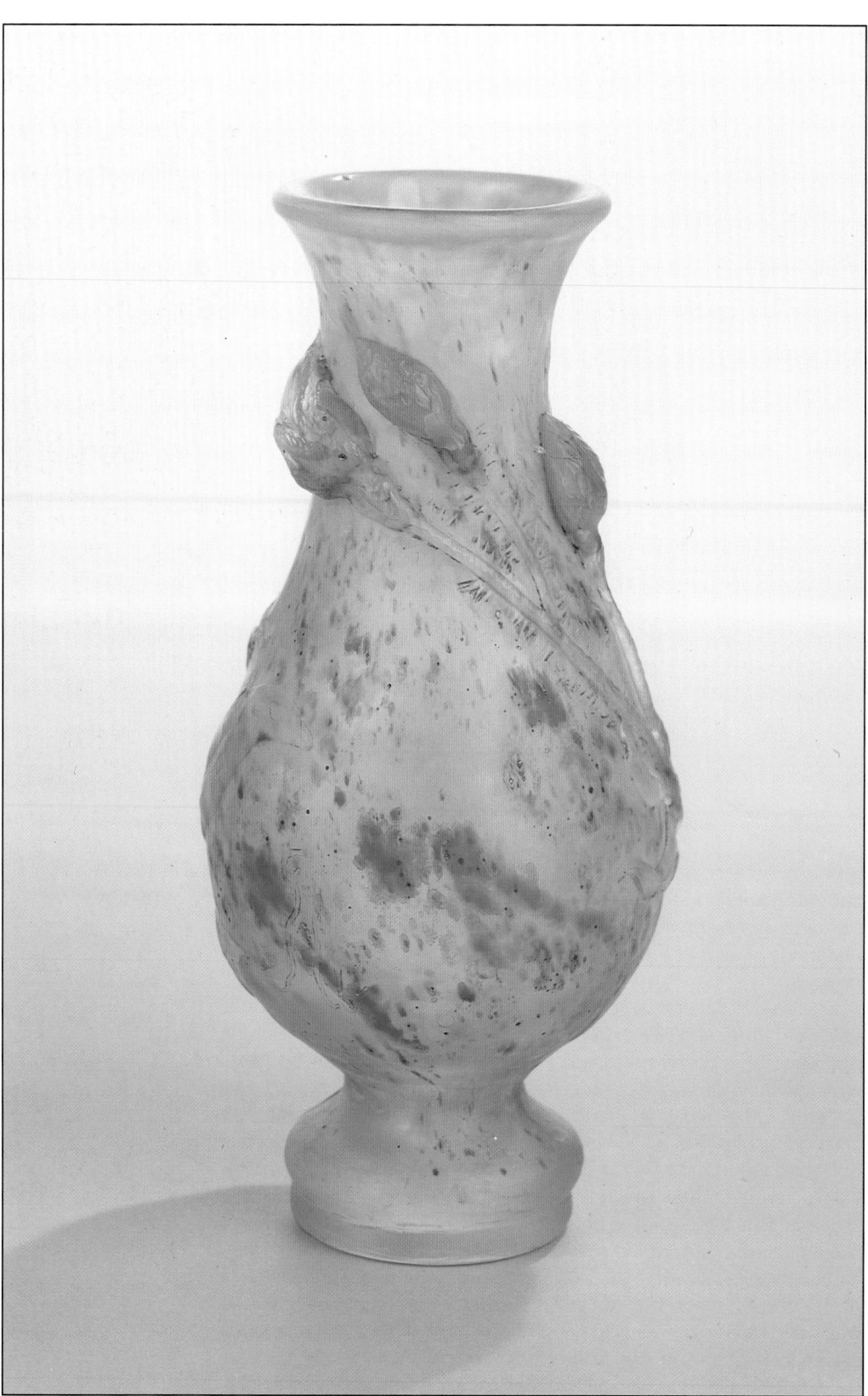

LEFT *Crocuses* vase, 1900, *marqueterie de verre* and then engraved, 13in/35cm high.

ABOVE Cameo vases, *c*.1900, featuring from left to right, chrysanthemums, oak leaves, acorns, and dragonflies above a lily pond.

OPPOSITE A mould-blown vase with clematis, 9½in/24cm high.

found appreciation was a religion of nature, but a religion without a defined God, nearer to pantheism, sometimes even pagan, but always based on a deep love and respect for the world around him.

Gallé's own thoughts on the natural world are best expressed in the collection of his writings made after his death, *Ecrits pour l'Art*. The most extraordinary aspect of these is that a majority of them are not treatises on art and the techniques of his craft, but reviews of horticultural exhibitions he visited throughout France. Of the exhibits at the Concours Régional de la Floriculture in 1884, he wrote: 'Further along, hydrangeas spread out the majesty of their orb-like blossoms and gradations of exquisitely fresh shades, gentle turquoise faintly brushed with pale indigo, or snow white dotted with sapphire buds. Some, finely green and wan, their marvellous vastness tinged with lilac rose.' At such exhibitions, his attention was drawn by so many exotic sights that he had to remind himself of simpler pleasures. 'But who would prefer the flesh of the camellia to the heart of the rose with its simple bud, its eyes barely open, seeming to weep already at its fate. Allow someone who has, for far too long, sung the praises of anaemic plants, to love roses, and especially those roses which start life with a faded and lovingly moulded look. Long live the rose, the eternally adorable queen!' Gallé's extravagant language, particularly describing the colour of flowers, suggests an intoxication in the presence of such beauty; but it is also the attempt of an artist to memorize the subtle aspects of appearance he hopes to reproduce in his work.

IRIS

In his Ecrits, Gallé tells us a strange story of a man in search of true
happiness. The man asks a flower where he should go. The flower
tells him to look at night at the stars, but the stars tell him to hurry
back to the flower. In Iris, Gallé plays with this idea, combining an
engraved blue iris against a dark blue-green background speckled
with light flecks like stars against the sky. On the reverse of the vase,
the same iris is shown wilted, curling off its stem, introducing a
melancholy note.

Iris, c.1895–1900, a blown and
cased vase with additional staining,
internal patination and engraved.
Including bronze base, 12½in/33cm
high.

ABOVE Vase with gilded base,
c.1900, 5in/13cm high.

Gallé visited famous gardens throughout Europe. In 1878, he travelled to the Troubetzkoi Villa in northern Italy, with its remarkable gardens set on Lake Maggiore. 'At the villa', he remembered, 'purely scientific satisfaction is accompanied by the keenest enjoyment offered to an artist enamoured of the enchantment of nature. Strangers abound and are welcome in the most open manner. A simple visiting card opens the doors of this Eden.' That same year he also visited the Isola Madre, one of the Borromean islands in Lake Maggiore, of which he wrote: 'This is not a dead woman in her wreath of flowers, it is a real island, truly alive. Neither is it Robinson's island. Fénelon [François Fénelon (1651–1715), a French theologian and defender of quietism, a form of religious mysticism] would have been the one more likely to be charmed by its grottoes of ferns, its groves of fig trees. He would have set Calypso on its soft meadows, iridescent with anemones, violets and hyacinths. One fine, sandy beach, beneath silver willows,

would be worthy of Ulysses and Nausicaä. There, Phoebus still hurls his arrows into the radiant undergrowth. Further off, Olympus shines through a haze of amber and gold, an Olympus with rich terraces covered with lemon trees, with glorious buds of Erythrina and Salvia – flowering laurels with their white blossoms bringing to mind Ovid's *Metamorphoses.* This shade, under the cypresses and the evergreen oaks, is this not Elysian?' Gallé's rich hyperbole stretches towards poetry, combining the names of flowers with those of pagan Gods.

It was in the work of writers and poets that Gallé sought a clarification of his feelings about nature. 'Baudelaire has expressed for us most grandly,' he wrote, 'the concept of creation's harmony of resonances.' He then quoted a verse from the poet. 'Nature is a temple where living pillars/Sometimes let slip confused words./ Man passes there through a forest of symbols/ Which watch him with familiar glances.' It was these symbols that Gallé liked to interpret on his glassware and furniture. 'Indeed, love of nature,' he concluded, 'must always lead to symbolism. The popular flower loved by all will always occupy a principal role in ornamental symbolism.'

It is in the late 1880s that we first see Gallé's philosophy applied directly to his glassware. In *Magnolia*, a vase dated 1889, he portrays the magnolia blossom in white enamel on clear glass with the branches and buds engraved. Other colours are also present in the glass, more like stains, giving it an intriguing atmosphere. 'Where the gold precipitate has marked the sodium based glass with spots of blue, violet, currant-red, chestnut brown and earthy brown,' he noted, 'this effect is meant to imitate the colours of the scales and petals that curl about the buds and blossoms of the magnolia.'

In 1893, Gallé produced a clear glass ewer with the shape and tinted colours of Roman glass. Looking closer, we see he is illustrating a hazel tree in subtle colours. His own description of it reveals the depths of meaning in his work: 'Clear crystal ewer, agatized by oxidation, with iridescent refraction and purpurine transparency. The engraving suspends the flower of the nut tree in all its nuances to the pouch which is beaded with blonde reflections. Pollen spreads a sulphurous cloud on the ruby stigmata and future hazelnuts. The anxiety of influorescences, whorls and pendants become wind blown in the rude awakening of February. The oblique sleet, the blue-tinged vapours, rainbowed, melt on the branches, dripping into liquid pustules, in ripping tears of crystal and silver: first laughter of the year, uncertain hope, premature decoration.'

Orchids always sent Gallé into a riot of metaphors. 'The orchids of that eminent grower, Crousse, those jewels of pure freshness, of pleasant peculiarity, of strange wonder . . . *Cochylodes* where the coral and the brightest scarlet fade under a spark of unexpected blue, sombre *Laelia*, sly *Cypripedium*, fluttering of *Oncidium*, all moving like octopi perceived under the water of an aquarium, flowers grown indifferent to the cries of ecstasy . . .' The exuberance of this passage is matched by two vases of around 1900. On one, the life cycle of the flower is followed from its vibrant pink bloom to languid, drooping leaves. The flowers on this have been hot-moulded separately, then attached as a piece of relief sculpture to a blue-violet base. On a second vase, exquisite white petals are splayed against a honeycomb amber vase.

OPPOSITE A dragonfly coupe, 1903, blown glass with applied details and metallic foil inclusions, 7½in/19cm high.

ABOVE Dragonfly coupe, 1903, reverse view.

PINES

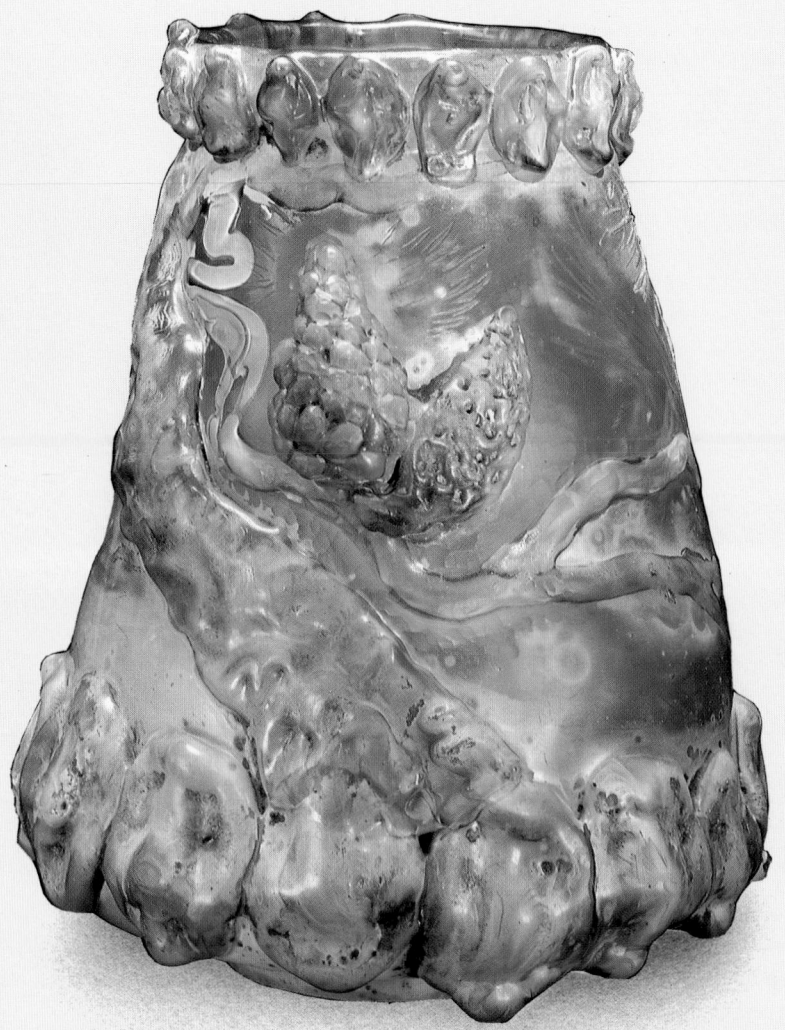

Pine trees are powerfully architectural, dark verticals against the horizon, funereal in their stance. Gallé took hold of these qualities in a series of vases like urns. In a squat, solid vase, he treats the details of the pine as encrustations, so the whole is as knobbly as a pine cone, asking to be touched. Pine needles are sketchily engraved like an impressionistic portrait of them. In a taller, more elegant vase, the mass of colours is calmed, becoming a liquid green, like resin. A branch curves round the vase, its pine cone more like grapes on a Roman sarcophagus with needles delicately fanning out in the glass, quiet and sombre.

Pines, 1903, a blown glass vase with
marquetry and applied detail,
7in/18cm high.

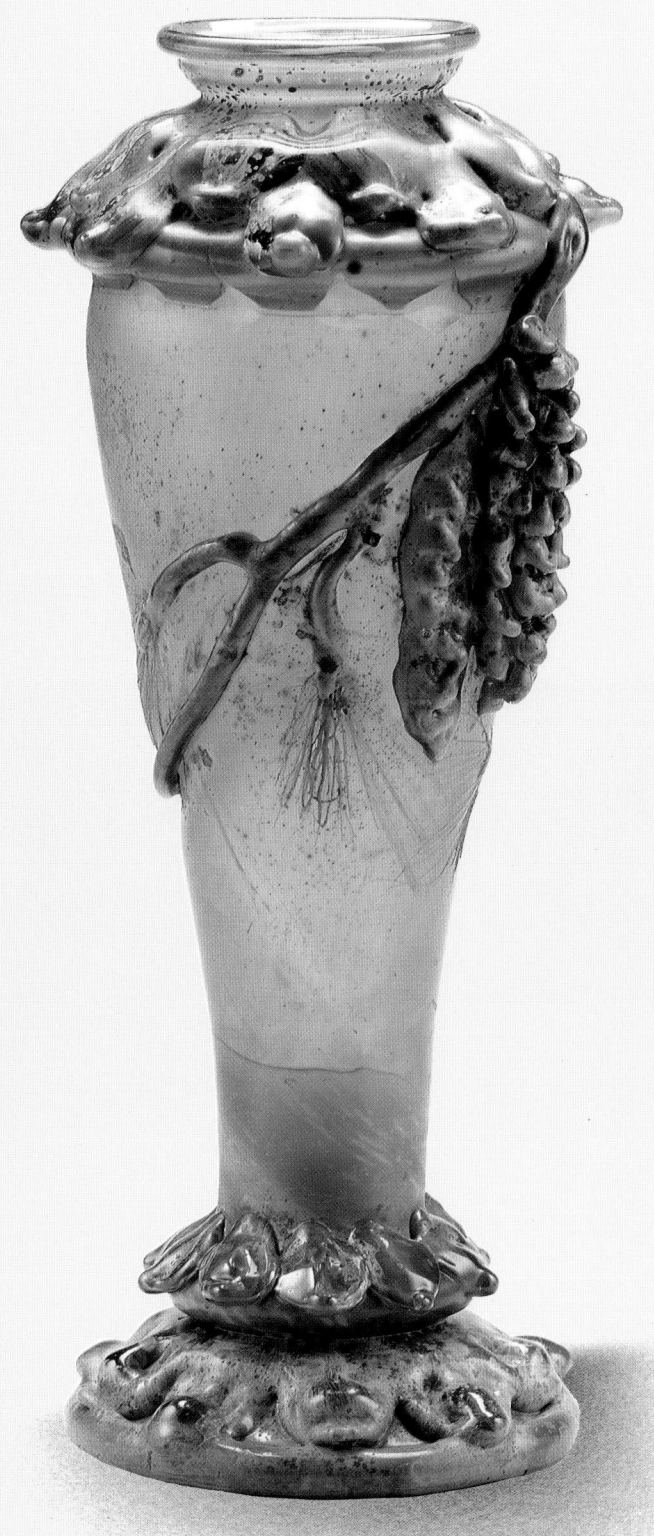

A pine cone vase, c.1902–3,
mould-blown with marquetry and
applied detail, 16½in/43cm high.

RIGHT Beetle and forest floor goblet, with immature beetles on base, 7in/20cm high.

LEFT An Egyptian-style vase, c.1900.

In *Violet*, Gallé forms an entire *coupe* (goblet) out of a single mould-blown blossom. Such is the magnification of this single flower that the actual veins of the living flower are shown, from its purple tip spout back to its colourless body. Gallé applied a similar idea to a *coupe* shaped from a rhubarb leaf, while on the side he engraved the entire plant. The leaves of the plant go on to form the base of the *coupe* as well as making a handle from the twist of a leaf. Meissonnier, the great Rococo craftsman, would have recognized a similar mind to his own in this piece. A later vase, *Barley*, is perhaps the last word in Gallé's creation of form suggested by plant shapes. A thin, elegant vase, it follows the shape of a head of barley, gently swelling from its base to its narrow neck, carrying the model of its shape as an engraved red stalk.

Flowers were certainly Gallé's favourite natural symbol, and particularly suited to the medium of vases, but the rest of the natural world was a great inspiration and it was not long before he was experimenting with animal shapes, especially insects. Almost at once, he resolved the problem of incorporating a dragonfly on a vase so it seemed integrated with the glass and not merely a random motif attached to it. The inspiration for this must have come from studying prehistoric dragonflies caught in pine resin and thus fossilized in amber. The most beautiful example of a whole series of dragonfly objects is a goblet of 1903. In this, a realistically portrayed dragonfly with speckled wings and body is embedded in cameo-like glass with two metallic eyes glinting from the milky background. the veins of the wings are engraved, while the insertion of silvery metallic foil adds natural lustre to them.

Having mastered this fossilized containment for his dragonflies, Gallé became bolder when dealing with other insects which did not lend themselves so easily to this conceit. In a beetle vase of 1900, he takes the potentially grotesque image of a giant rhinoceros beetle scavenging among decaying leaves, and transforms it into an intriguing, if not exactly beautiful, work in which the body of the vase is made of a deep jade glass dappled to represent a murky jumble of leaves on the forest floor. As for the beetle, its presence may be similar to that of another beetle described by Gallé in his *Ecrits*:

> *We do not know the name of the fine, thoughtful artist, sculptor of Egypt, royal goldsmith, magus or decorator of temples who, having stopped to observe the action of a filthy insect – the dung beetle – as it fashioned a ball of dung to deposit its eggs in the warmth of the Libyan sand, was touched by a kind of religious awe. He was the first apparently to discover the reflection of an august image, to invent the mystic jewel – the sacred scarab. The frong legs of this insect – and later, in Phoenician imitations, its spread wings – support the solar globe, the origin of light and warmth. While in its hind legs, it maternally rolls another celestial globe, the earth, into which it deposits the seeds of life. What remarkable testimony by the artist–inventor to the existence of a Divine Creator, to the providential bringing together of a planet with its source of heat! Strange and ancient prescience, one might say, of the planetary form of the earth itself. Here is a symbol of art, cosmography, religion and prophecy.*

RIGHT Cameo vases, *c.*1900, showing the range of Gallé's botanical interests, including an example of seaweed, on the far left.

ABOVE Walnut and fruitwood
marquetry étagère, 30in/76cm high.

This is a remarkable passage. Gallé clearly admires the vision of the anonymous Egyptian who transformed an essentially repulsive creature into a symbol of life and the world. A symbol that is not just artistic, but religious too. This was what Gallé aspired to, devoting his career to the establishment of new symbols from the natural world. It is a grand ambition, full of innocent enthusiasms, and one that imbues his work with charm at its least successful, and at its best, comes close to the religious awe he described.

To explore the idea of time, Gallé began a series of vases in 1889 in which tadpoles become frogs as they swim up the muddy glass sides. At the top of the vase, he inscribed a verse by Théophile Gautier: 'Upon the moats, the duckweed/ With its leaves of verdigris/ Extends a curtain of sea-green.' These short lines have the quality of Japanese *haiku* poems, which had only just caught the imagination of Western writers. These intensely short poems were intended to conjure up a

single image of contemplation on nature, an image resonating beyond its mere details. Such an idea coincided with Gallé's own view of nature and the inscriptions on his vases should be seen in this light, creating the mood of his composition.

From the animal world, Gallé moved even further away from traditional decorative subject matter. In *Geology*, a vase created about 1900, he used the world of natural science, portraying the formation of crystals. From the top of the translucent vase, drops of liquid chemicals roll down towards the base where they form rhomboids of what might be calcite, malachite and azurite. It is a unique piece, both in subject and finish, evoking the pleasure of rich crystal and yet composed out of relatively inexpensive glass. The climax of this particular strand of work came with Gallé's goblet made at the request of the Ecole-Normale Supérieure in Paris in 1893 to celebrate the 70th birthday of the great scientist, Louis Pasteur.

THE PASTEUR GOBLET

At first sight, the Pasteur goblet appears a simple, rather crude shape, heavily engraved. But as one looks closer, a whole world of microscopic detail is revealed. Gallé accompanied the goblet to Pasteur with a booklet several pages long to describe all the engraved detail. He called it his 'innoculated' glass, and it must surely be the only objet d'art ever created to feature micro-organisms in its decoration. The portrayal of microbes is based on plates in biology textbooks. The extent of Gallé's research and his attempt to combine the reality of Pasteur's achievement with his own natural symbolism are revealed in one of the passages from his manuscript explaining the decoration of the vase. The 'Master' he refers to is Pasteur:

'Beneath the amber penumbra lie gloomy reminders of a sick chicken, a sinister dog foaming at its mouth, fixed emblems of the casualties that you, Master, to your glory, have explored. Just as you have proved the relation to their respective effects of the virus swimming among globules of blood, germs carried on the atmosphere, elegant sporulations of Saccharomyces Pastorianus, symmetrical strangulation of the bacteria in your micrococcus cholerae galinarum as they are split in two, the dreaded Pasteur micrococcus, the spirilla of stagnant water, the decorative parasite of malarial infections, the pneumonia staphylococcus, the coloration of the violet bacillus. Forms that are shaped like a rosary, the whitish colonies of cultures on plates. . . . Inside the vase, the branches, rootlets, or barbs of gathered feathers try to imitate the development of certain cultures injected into gelatin. But the colour yellow is an error due to the defective chromolithography in a manual.'

The breadth and sustained detail of Gallé's decorative scheme for this goblet, even to the point of admitting a mistake in his micro-biology, must be the final word in 19th-century artistic naturalism.

The Pasteur goblet, 1892, etched
with microbes and medicinal plants.
Made of blown and cased glass,
engraved and probably acid-
etched, it stands 9½in/25cm high.

OPPOSITE *Etagère à la Japonica,*
with its uprights carved in imitation
bamboo.

By the 1890s, in France and the rest of Europe, Art Nouveau had moved away from imitative naturalism to a greater degree of abstraction. The flower and the leaf were abandoned as the stem, with its pure line, set the aesthetic standard for turn-of-the-century design. Modernism was beginning to develop, and the Belgian designer Henri Van de Velde (1863–1957) summed up the new direction: 'The relation between the ornament and the form or the surfaces should appear so intimate that the ornament seems to have determined the form.' Gallé could always agree with this – his decoration was not appended as an afterthought. The form of his objects was determined by their subject matter in often imaginative and daring ways, but he would not follow the path towards abstraction and pure Art Nouveau. By 1900, he was a confirmed naturalist and can really be seen as an artist separate from the spirit of the time, pursuing his own interests and beliefs. This is the strength of his work. It always sprang from a personal vision, rather than the dictates of art or fashion.

In his writings, Gallé makes clear the inspiration for his furniture, in this case, wood mouldings: 'Take directly the peduncula of the leaf or the flower of the *Orchidea*, the *Umbellifer* of our woods. Study the striations which furrow them. They are alternatively thick and thin. Examine them with strong magnification. They have the look of true cabinetmaker's or architect's mouldings, with lights opposed to shades, roundnesses to planes. . . . Here and there is it interrupted regularly, masterfully, by the insertion of leaves and branches. To learn the secret of these combinations, take cuttings, multiply the sketches, but compare them to the living model. You will be surprised to find these anatomies increasingly full of charms and secrets, always superior in beauty to the adaptations based on them. You will be surprised that man has so little delved into this infinite repertory to renew his art of furniture.'

Gallé first discovered wood in 1885. He wanted an elegant table to show off his glassware and decided to design it himself. When he entered a shop in Nancy specializing in rare woods, he was enchanted. The scents of the different types, their exotic patterns of grain and subtle shades of colour fed his imagination. 'I discovered India and America', he exclaimed. Gallé had no experience in woodworking, but within the year he had a fully equipped factory of expert cabinetmakers. His good friend Victor Prouvé provided assistance with the furniture designs and together they created some remarkable objects.

At first, the form of their furniture was determined by previous styles. They produced solid chests and tables in the form of Renaissance furniture with thick columns and heavily carved surfaces. They let their enthusiasm for materials run away, creating a *grand meuble d'appui* layered with exotic veneers and a slab of marble – though even here, on its drawers, were included details of insects in exquisite marquetry. Shelved cabinets with glass doors for displaying his vases were a favourite item, and in these Gallé displayed his more obvious Oriental influences. An *étagère à la Japonica* had open woodwork in the form of blossom hanging low over the shelves, while its four uprights were carved in imitation bamboo. The lightness of touch in this was repeated in other cabinets of the 1890s, whose branches and

stems swing asymmetrically across them, as they balance on slim legs copied exactly from budding stems. The marquetry in all these objects is breathtaking in its complexity and natural detail; Gallé kept at least 600 different kinds of veneers in his factory.

In 1892, Gallé designed a dining table for Henri Vasnier, one of the Champagne family of Pommery in Reims. It was called *La Table aux Herbes Potagères*, literally the Pot-Herb Table. As with his glassware, Gallé was getting closer and closer to the ideas he wanted to express about nature and its relationship to man. He began his description of the table by saying, 'the very simple form of this piece of furniture was dictated by its purpose, which also suggested the decorative theme of the pot-herbs.' He then goes on to say that having left behind other decorative styles, he has developed his own based on the attractive forms of vegetables such as cabbage and chicory. He chose marquetry as the best way of representing them, for having once been living wood itself it expressed the life force of the subject. Also, as an artist he found that, 'wood offers a much wider range of colours than you might think, some of them quite breathtaking . . . you will find here the deep purple of Labaka wood on the flat surface . . . the blue of the Winter cabbage, the tinged shoots of the asparagus, spotted with its berries, and the male and female pumpkin.'

Gallé ran through a list of vegetables and herbs, all represented in the marquetry of the table or its very structure. 'For this table, you will see I have made little columns in the forms of *Legumineuses* and gourd branches, the herb creepers intertwine a little, twisting, as they encroach on the edges of the table; the cucumber tendrils embracing it, delicious and tortuous.' It is a *tour de force* and Gallé concludes his description with the passage quoted at the beginning of the chapter, expressing his gratitude for the plant world and the sustenance it provides for mankind.

The next year, Gallé took his appreciation of vegetables and fruit a step further, defining for them a firm list of symbolic meanings. In *Les Fruits de l'Esprit* of 1893, Gallé designed a tall chest as a gift from the parish of Bischwiller to their pastor Daniel Grimm in celebration of his 50 years in the post. The pastor was also Gallé's father-in-law so he lavished particular affection on it, and it seems to have brought him to focus on his Protestant background and somehow combine it with his less orthodox passion for nature. For the structure of the piece he chose the classical details of early Christian architecture. The primitive Christian nature of this article,' he explained, 'is accentuated by its construction. It consists of an aedicule [a shrine or other opening framed by two columns] surmounted by a grill-fronted loggia. The square, haloed cross on the top arises from a denticulated pediment and the bronze decoration forms Christ's monogram . . . In the lower part, we see the field of corn calling the workers at harvest time. The knobs of the drawers open in *Cruciferae* flowers with four petals chiselled in the pierced bronze.'

As in the previous piece, Gallé is at pains to use the variety of woods available to him to best effect. 'It is the colour, or should I say, the shading which gives the symbols their real prestige. The colours provide the setting and create the mysterious atmosphere wherein the vibrant,

OPPOSITE Table lamp, *c.*1900.

RIGHT *Meuble à musique* (music holder), *c.*1900, made of fruitwood marquetry and decorated with butterflies.

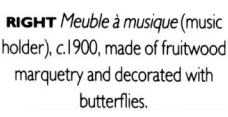

LEFT Display case, *c.*1900, with carved butterflies and fruitwood marquetry.

RIGHT *Aube et Crépuscule*
(*Dawn and Dusk*), 1904, the bed
Gallé designed for his friend Henri
Hirsch, and which is now in the
Musée de L'Ecole de Nancy
alongside Gallé's lamp, *Les Coprins*
(*Ink Caps*).

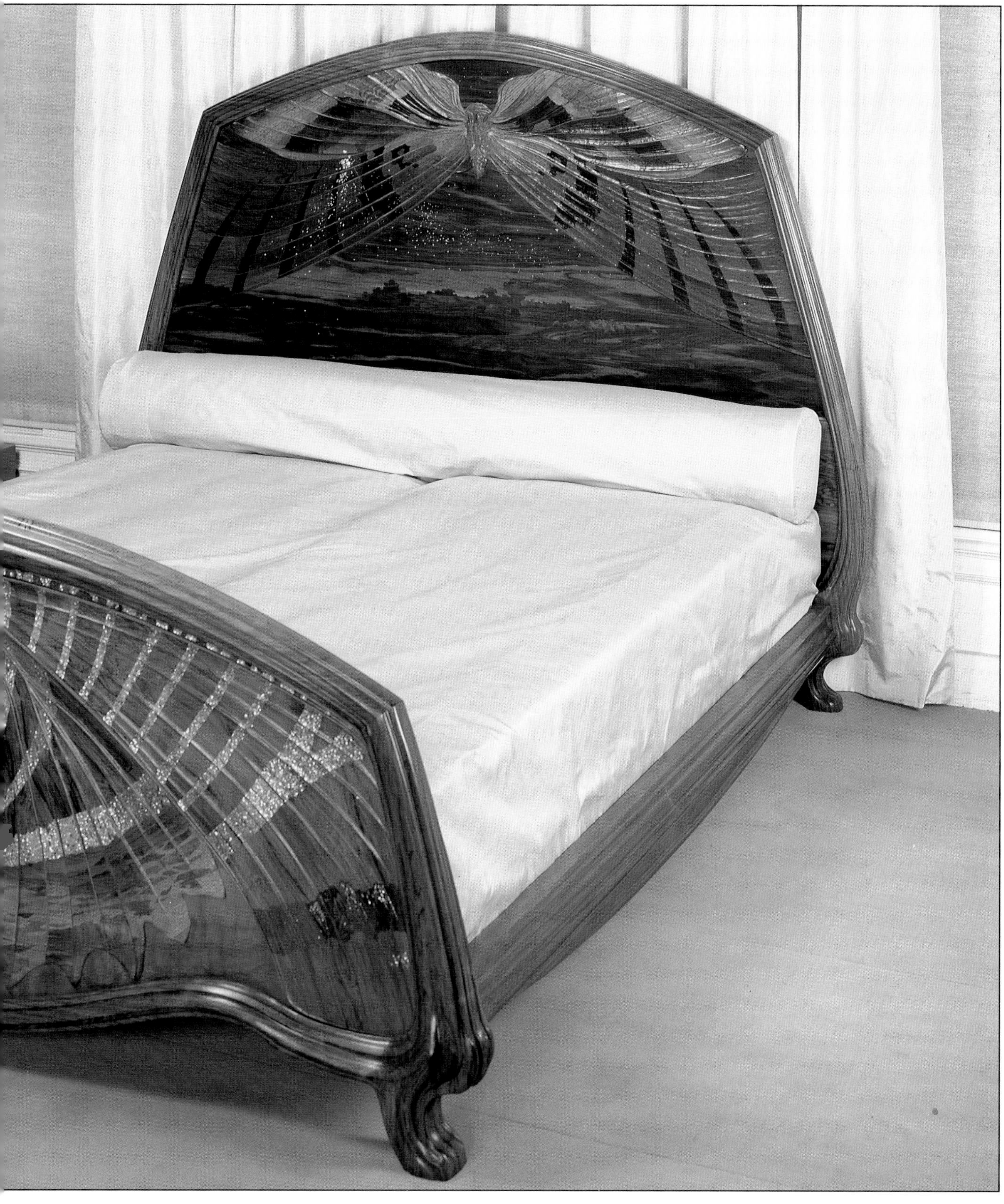

divine texts are to be inscribed. Further, the artist-cabinetmaker, wishing to express through wooden materials an immaterial vision of future and distant things, has taken care not to employ the precision and polish of 18th-century cabinetmakers. He has left the velvet finish of a tapestry on his marquetry woods . . . Elsewhere, matt colours seem to paraphrase the holy text in the flexible language of the island wood: May your evening be like a golden morning! . . . At the bottom, the cedar of Lebanon and the cypress, badge of numerous, green years. These trees are powdery like the pallor of old frescoes.' This passage shows the thought behind Gallé's every decision on how and when to use a particular wood.

Finally, Gallé explains the title of the piece, neatly tying together his Christian agricultural symbolism. 'The fruits of the spirit', said St. Paul, 'are charity, joy, peace, patience, kindness, goodness, faithfulness, gentleness and moderation.' *Les Fruits de l'Esprit* flower in a cornucopia of fecundity and symbols, not on a horizon where the sun is sinking, but in a dawn sky. Charity and kindness are depicted in the mystical corn. Grapes represent the symbolic blood of the Eucharist. Peace is shown by the olive branch, its silver leaves hanging from the dove's beak on the independent cupboard doors. Gentleness has as its symbol the fruit of the generous fig-tree, temperance, that of the date. Goodness is the altruistic bee, always harvesting for others. Joy is the myrtle, while the narcissus and the dandelion are Spring and the rebirth of absolution for our souls. Faithfulness is the flower Veronica, the Christian lamp, the night-light which has beaten back the shadow through a long night and whose flame will be found burning, vigilant at daybreak.'

Marquetry in three dimensions was a dramatic effect developed in Gallé's workshop, reflecting his desire for even greater naturalism. A firescreen of 1900, shown at the Exposition Universelle, is a simple but striking example. From the frame of the screen curls a serpentine creeper, carved against a background of marquetry illustrating the same plant but in lighter wood, thus creating a sense of depth which is carried on by the grain of the wood evoking a landscape beyond that. The most extraordinary display of both Gallé's imagination and the skill of his woodwork factory, however, was his bed, *Aube et Crépuscule* (Dawn and Dusk), designed in 1904 and intended to celebrate the wedding of a close friend and patron, Henri Hirsch.

The end of the bed and the headboard were dominated by huge moths with outspread wings portrayed in a rich mix of veneers. Most exotic of all were the bands of mother-of-pearl mosaic laid into their wings to recreate their silvery sheen. The jaws of the giant moth at the end of the bed held a large oval drop of glass, itself etched with moths. Beneath the wings of the moth on the bedhead was a night landscape depicted in an array of fruitwood marquetry with gold-dust seemingly scattered over it by the moth. For Gallé, this must have been intended as a symbol of night and the flight of dreams represented by the moths. To its newly married owners, however, it may have seemed sinister, bordering on the nightmarish. It is an indication of the brooding mood in Gallé's later works, wherein a dark symbolism overcomes his optimistic pleasure in the natural world.

LEFT Bedhead of *Aube et Créspuscule*, showing a moth and a night landscape in fruitwood marquetry and dust of mother-of-pearl.

CHAPTER FOUR
TECHNIQUE

ABOVE AND RIGHT Vases and
table lamp, *c.*1900, typical of the
glassware produced in Gallé's
factory both during his lifetime and
after his death.

For all great designers whose work identifies an epoch, it is not enough simply to create the individual works, however magnificent they are. The complete success derives from manufacturing the goods on a mass scale, maintaining a high quality and marketing them widely. Many of the objects illustrated in this book were single commissions mady by Gallé for special occasions and favoured patrons, but he also oversaw the production of more ordinary glassware in his factory destined for shops throughout France, Great Britain, Germany and North America. It was the profit from these successful lines that underwrote Gallé's expensive experiments in the chemistry of glass. His frequent showings at international exhibitions in Paris were intended not only to impress a minority of art critics, but to create publicity and fuel demand from retailers.

In Nancy, Gallé paid special attention to the environment and organization of his workers. Like other far-sighted capitalists of the 19th century, he believed strongly that an efficient and stimulating workplace was of vital importance to high production standards. A contemporary description of his workshops emphasizes the pleasant environment he created:

> *The factory is surrounded by tall trees creating an atmosphere of peace and calm. At the right time of year, in the centre of the courtyard, beds of flowers delight the eye while providing a constant source of education for your [Gallé's] personnel. In the main building, a model of true architectural elegance, the work is divided methodically. In one room, the cabinetmakers select, assemble, cut and apply the thin strips of precious wood that will decorate tables, consoles, jewellery cases, mirrors and other furniture of all shapes kept in the next studio. In another room, craftsmen prepare the models and painters decorate the faïenceware that will be placed into a series of kilns, from which bellies of fire they emerge in full splendour. Elsewhere, spindles and engraving wheels score and flute glass, enriching it with the finest engravings. Further on, specialists cast, chisel and patinate the bronze mounts that complete items of furniture. Then, in an enormous hall, are a number of furnaces liquefying the glass that powerful lungs or the pressure of moulds will transform into vases, bowls, goblets and the thousand of fantasies that have earned your glasswork its well-deserved celebrity.*

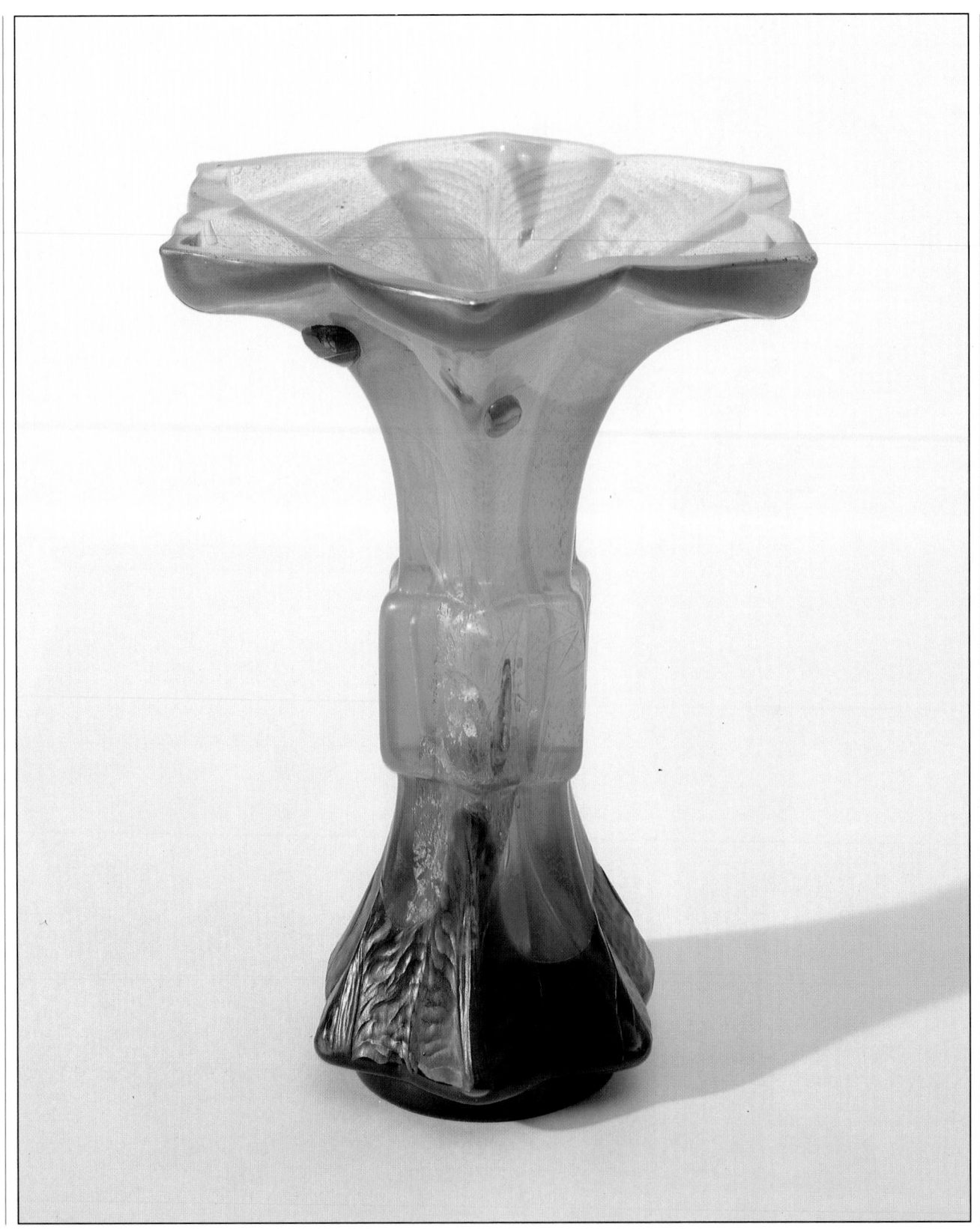

ABOVE Enamelled vases, c.1890–1900.

OPPOSITE A carved and applied glass vase, c.1900, standing 9in/23cm high.

At the time of this description, c.1900, Gallé employed about 300 workmen. In addition to the natural inspiration planted by the flowerbeds around his factory, Gallé provided them with a well-stocked library. All the workshops were well lit, with water and gas supplies and a central heating system. Gallé was also interested in monitoring the performance of his employees, and introduced a scheme for calculating the hours of labour. Workers on private commissions were given white cards, while those producing the normal factory output had coloured cards. The cards provided day-by-day information on progress so that at the end of the work session the office staff could check how many hours had been worked by each craftsman and add this to the cost of the product.

Gallé treated his management of the factory as a matter of philosophy. He was determined not to repeat the mistakes of the 19th century with its degrading industrialism. He shared a desire for a utopian concept of virtuous labour similar to that held by William Morris (1834–1896), whom he called 'a prophet of the joy in work'. In his *Ecrits* he wrote: 'This was one of the errors, one of the bitter penalties of the age of industrialism, of the excessive division of labour, of its organization far from the domestic fireplace, the family and the natural environment. Instead, it put it in a postponed, artificial atmosphere. The century just past does not have its truly popular art, no art applied to useful objects and executed spontaneously, joyously, by the artisans of each craft.' It is not surprising, then, that Gallé should situate his factory next to his home and devote as much attention to its gardens as his own.

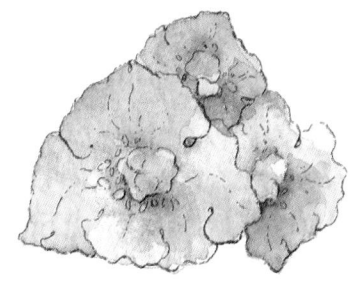

OPPOSITE Chalcedony-like glass vase with bubbles.

Although Gallé's signature appeared on all his major works, he was not slow to recognize the assistance of others in design and manufacture. His closest colleague was Victor Prouvé, the little boy he befriended when he first worked in his father's factory. They grew up together and it was Prouvé who painted the affectionate portrait of Gallé in his studio which now hangs in the Musée de l'Ecole de Nancy. Prouvé provided many of the sketches for the design of Gallé's furniture and was credited specifically with the designs of two of his major glassworks. On *Orpheus and Eurydice*, a vase of directly mythological imagery, he is credited as 'Friend, inventor of images, and fine painter', while on the *Joan of Arc* vase he is again mentioned as a friend and creator of the images of the embattled warrior saint. It appears that whenever human figures had to be portrayed, it was Prouvé, the professional artist, who possessed the skill to render them.

Gallé's inventive talent lay in his ability as an alchemist, conjuring up new colours to tint his glass and new processes for sealing the achievements. He went to great lengths to protect his ideas and explain them to judges of exhibition competitions, often referring to rivals latching on to his discoveries. In notes submitted to the jury of the Paris position Universal of 1889, he claims: 'I submitted for your consideration in 1878 a potassium-based glass coloured with a slight amount of cobalt oxide that produced an agreeable tone of sapphire. The decorative purpose to which I put this glass created a fashion for that shade. I marketed it under the name 'clair-de-lune' and it was reproduced subsequently in France, in England under the name of 'moonlight glass', and in Germany as 'Mondschein'. Since that time there is hardly a factory that has not manufactured 'clair-de-lune' and today it is in the public domain. Following my submission to the Union Centrale des Art Décoratifs in 1884, the same thing happened with contemporary manufacturers imitating the manner of my producing the yellowish tones of blonde oystershells misted over with red and blue hues. I had created these effects by projecting onto marble pounded opal and red glass with copper protoxide gathered around a hot gob of glass. These first experiments, still rather primitive, were regarded as a considerable success, but have now been surpassed by the numerous improvements I present to you today.'

Gallé goes on to describe a remarkable range of glass effects and the chemical combinations that produced them. He created yellows and iridescent greens from silver and sulphur, a peacock blue from copper and iron, and browns from sulphur and catechu. Trying to recreate the effect of amethyst quartz, he used manganese oxides, and then doused the glass in cold water to give it the cracks he admired in the crystal. A vase base is made with manganese and a layer of ruby crystal, then marbled with preparations including gold and silver. Jade is imitated with potassium-sulphate alabasters tinged with green by varying proportions of potassium bichromate and iron and copper oxides. Onyx agate is evoked by coloured ribbons of glass incorporated in clear cyrstal. Gallé liked to use bubbles in the glass to imitate raindrops or dew on the petals of orchids.

Faïence was the first medium Gallé experimented with. Under his father, he learned the basic principles of pottery and its decoration.

A NEW TECHNIQUE – MARQUETERIE DE VERRE

Many of Gallé's glassmaking techniques were his own variations on traditional skills, but marqueterie de verre *was completely his own invention. Inspired by his work on marquetry in wood, it is best defined as shaped pieces of hot glass pressed into the body of a glass object of contrasting colour with the resulting surface being flat. The inlaid pieces could then be further decorated with engraving or carving. In principle, it sounded simple, but in practise it was vulnerable to a great many hazards. The rates of expansion of each type of coloured glass were different, so Gallé had to select colours which would expand and contract at the same time, thus minimizing the possibility of cracking during the several stages of heating needed for each object. If in the last stages of heating, the class did crack, it was still considered a* chef d'oeuvres *but it was marked* Etude *(study) and kept in the workshop. Only the most perfect items went to exhibition. Gallé patented this technique in 1898.*

A glass bottle, coupe, and crocus
vase, all dating from c.1900, and
made from *marqueterie de verre.*

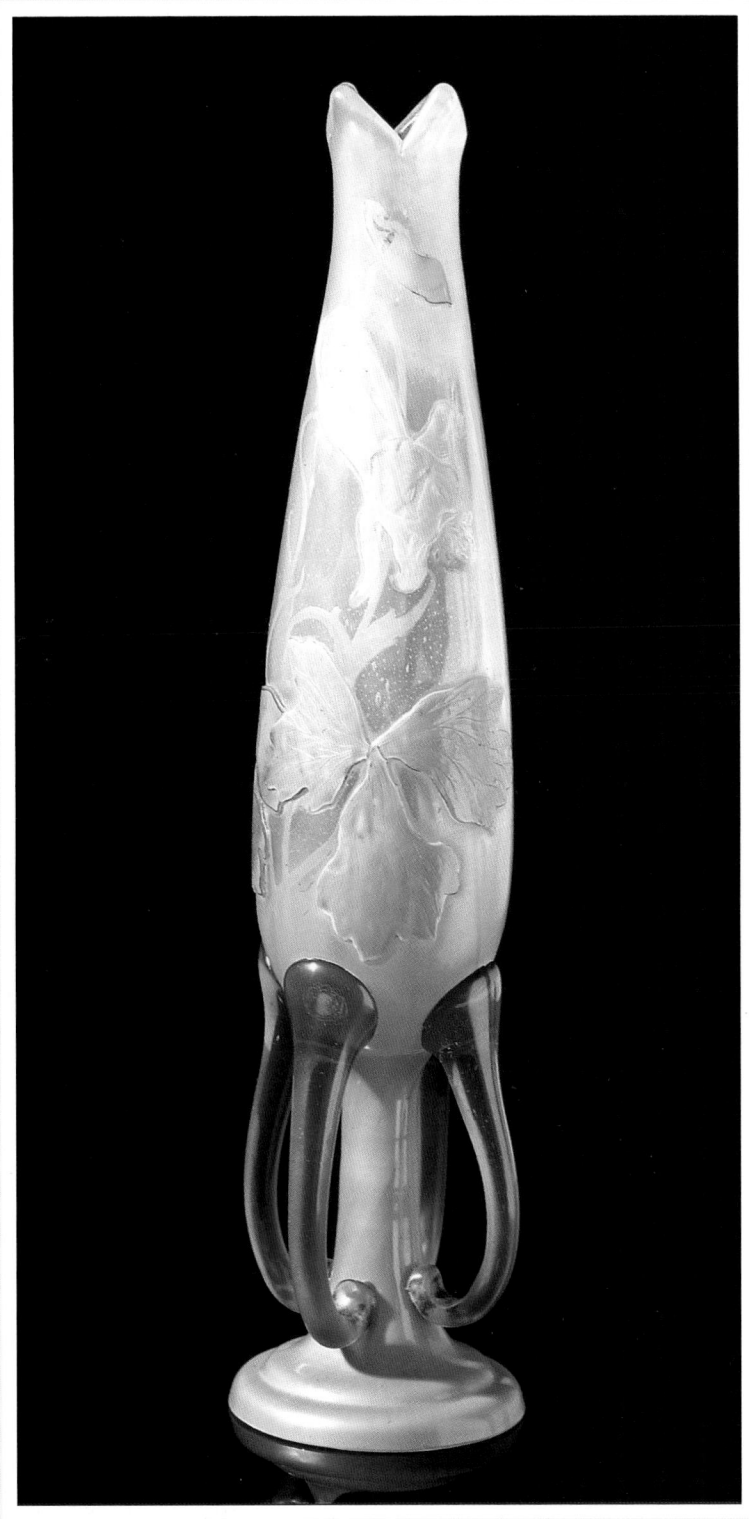

*Columbine, c.1902–4, a
marqueterie de verre* vase.

RIGHT Marbled glass bottle and stopper, engraved, *c*.1900.

OPPOSITE *Feuille de Chou* (*Cabbage Leaf*) coupe, *c*.1900, marbled and applied glass in the form of a cabbage leaf with butterflies engraved inside, 6in/ 16cm high.

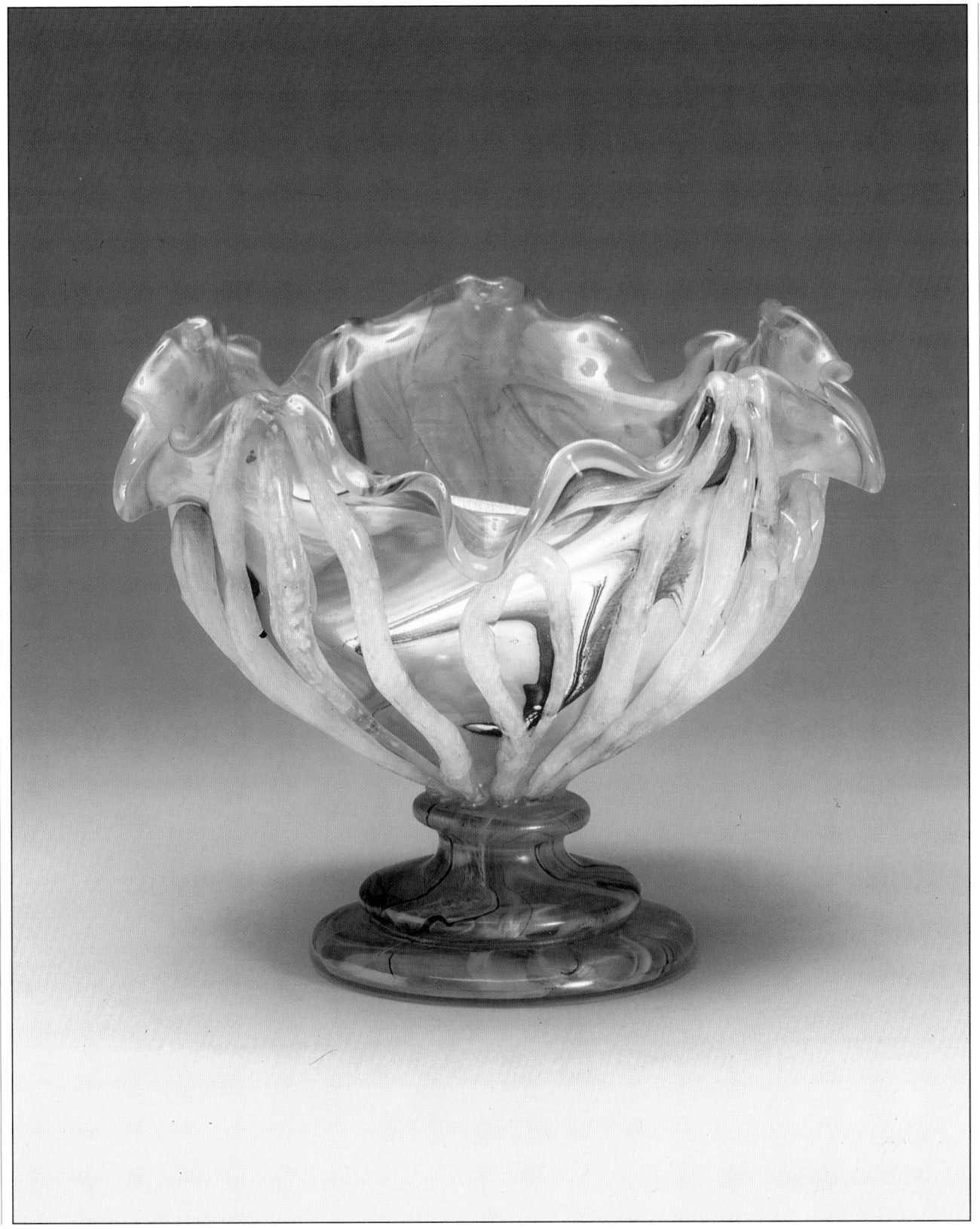

Using local clay, he perfected tin-based glazes, developing enamels and richer colours such as blue from cobalt oxide, green from copper oxide and other colours from chromium, iron or manganese oxides. He invented delicate effects like the speckling of a bird's egg and combinations of colour suspended in a semi-opaque glaze to give the illusion of velvet. Translucent enamels were painted over metal foils to replicate the richness of Limoges enamels. The resulting ceramics were bright and imaginative, but somewhat crude in their form, having a naïve rural quality about them. For Gallé, they ultimately lacked the sophistication he was developing in glass and he last exhibited his ceramics at the Salon du Champs-de-Mars in 1892.

ABOVE Glass plate for hanging on the wall, c.1900.

OPPOSITE Triple cameo vase, standing 33½in/85cm high.

CAMEO GLASS

Gallé's engraving of layered glass, giving the effect of cameo, was inspired by his 1871 visit to the British Museum in London, where he saw the Portland Vase. A Roman amphora of the 1st century AD, it is made of cobalt-blue translucent cased glass over which is a layer of white opaque glass carved in cameo relief. Cased glass is the result of fusing two moulded layers of different colours together and then cutting away at the top surface with an engraving wheel to produce the desired pattern set off by the glass beneath. Gallé adapted this method to his own glassware, creating an entire landscape by introducing greater subtlety into the engraving. Moving away from a simple black and white cameo, he pared away at a translucent layer so the glass became a blend of its own colour and the colour of the glass layer beneath. On a three-layered vase, he could thus cut into a red layer on top of a blue layer to the point that the thinned glass took on a burgundy hue representing the autumnal leaves of trees. Behind this, cutting away at the blue on the top of the yellow base, he evoked the green of more distant trees, then thinning the blue even more he produced the brilliant turquoise of a mountain lake.

Cameo chandelier, c.1900,
20½in/52cm wide.

A cameo vase, made of *verrerie
parlante*, inscribed '*Beni soit le coin
sombre ou s'isolent nos coeurs –
Valmore*'.

RIGHT A double overlay, carved and acid-etched vase (left), with a carved and fire-polished vase on the right.

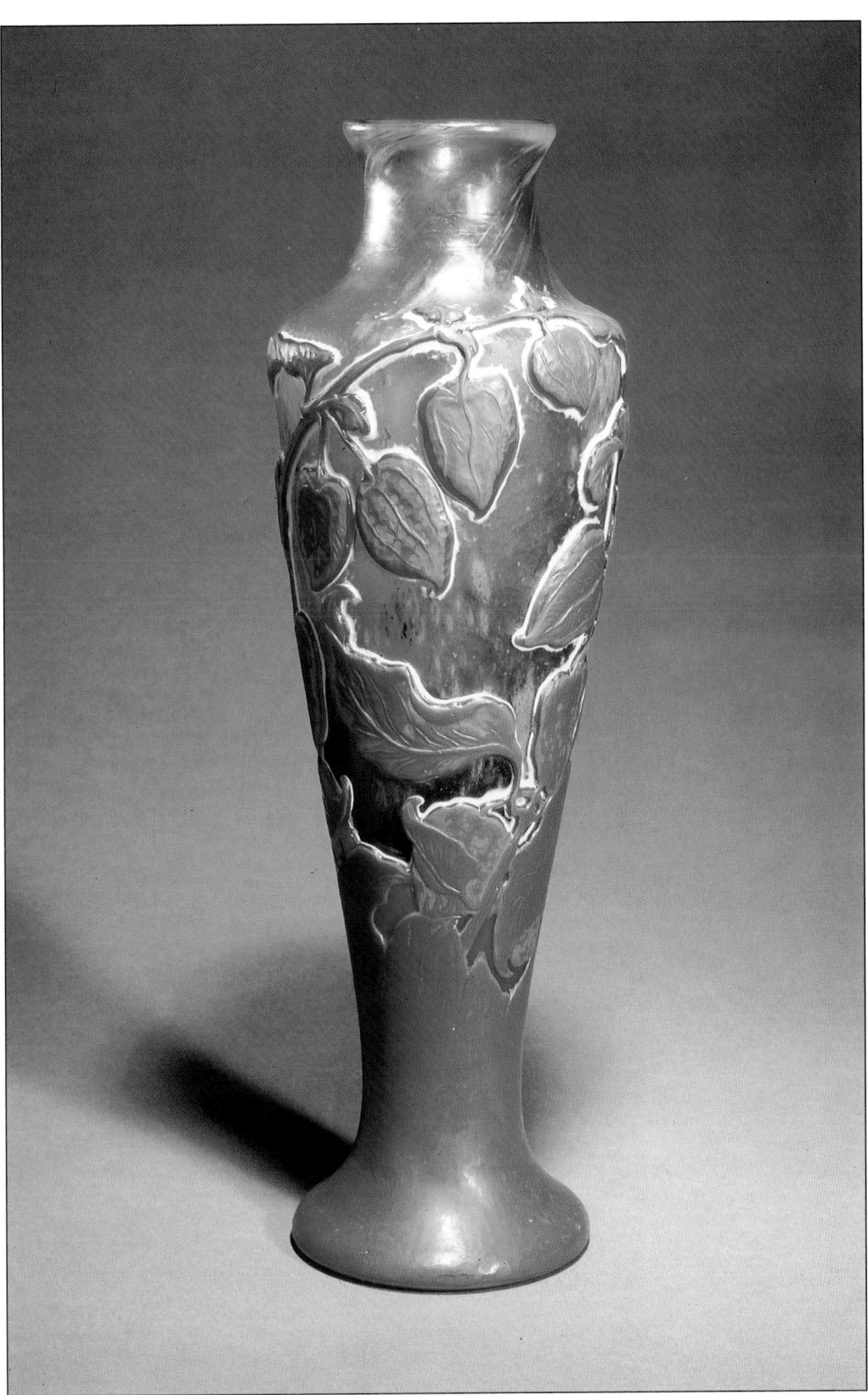

LEFT Quadruple overlay vase with
wheel carved decoration.

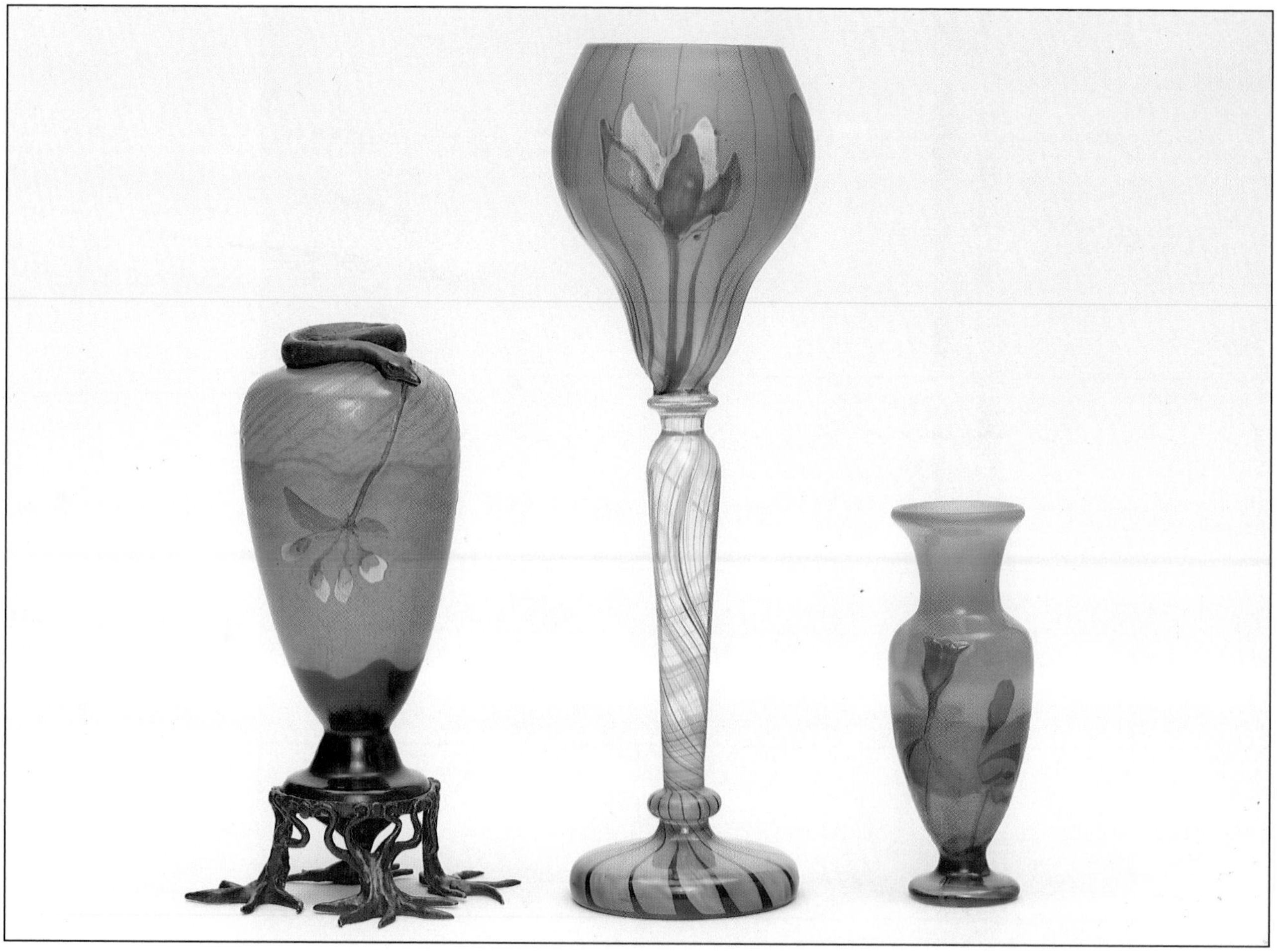

ABOVE Three vases, from c.1900; the vase on the left has a bronze base and the neck is encircled by a bronze snake.

OPPOSITE This cameo glass incense burner, 1900, is supported by silvered metal dragonflies.

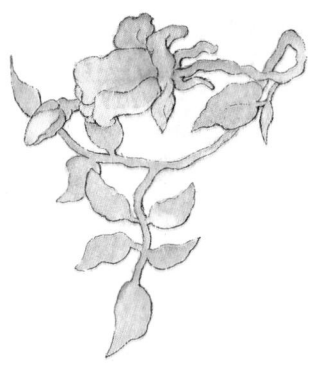

Patination was an accidental by-product of the glassmaking technique, but its effects soon became of interest to Gallé, as he explained in his application to patent a new technique in 1898: 'In the fabrication of glass or crystal, it often happens that the surface of the material is altered or contaminated while being worked in a paste state, the effect of being exposed to dusts from wood or coal combustion . . . Concerned about such defects, I had the idea of using them as a decorative means, by inducing the effect to obtain an entirely new type of decoration called patina. The dusts or ashes coming from the kiln and then embedded in the vitreous mass spread uniformly over the surface of the paste material, disturb, roughen and tear it in the working and thus modifies the surface so it comes to look like fabric, crêpe or a thick cobweb. To the touch it can seem to be either coarse or fine. It is this matt texture that I call *patine du verre*.'

Many of Gallé's most striking vases are virtually sculpture in glass. On these, fragments of broken coloured glass have been heated and applied to the warm base to form petals and leaves exquisitely folded, caressing the vase to which they have fused. This gave a marvellous illusion of depth. As one contemporary wrote: 'With nature's own grace, the applied flower seems to emerge from the depths of the

material, its parts adding relief to the object it decorates. Fine carving done with a small wheel has sharpened the contours and revealed the delicate nervation of petals.' In this way, Gallé added a beetle to a forest-dappled vase or a seahorse to a marine-coloured goblet. Engraving and etching, however, were vital to the complete effect, adding to the brilliant blob of coloured glass the texture and natural detail that enhanced the illusion.

Gallé's first engraved works were achieved with a small emery wheel or with lead, copper or wooden wheels. With these, he worked hard to create precise effects like precious intaglio work on gem stones. But Gallé tired of this, wanting looser, more impressionistic effects. He invented a vertical lathe to which he attached his wheels of different materials, each incizing to a different depth or texture. For the finishing touches and the signing of his name, hand tools were employed.

Etching provided Gallé with the ultimate in natural effects, although he also found its lack of control unsatisfying. The process involves covering the glass with an acid-resistant wax or varnish and then scratching into it with a sharp tool to form a design. A mixture of hydrofluoric acid, potassium flouride and water is then washed over it to corrode the exposed design into the body of the piece. The depth of the etching varies with the time of exposure. Seeing the increasing mastery of his glassworkers over the technique, Gallé used it to bite into glass creating the rough, random texture of bark or the subtle veining of leaves, or to etch flowers inside vases to surprise his clients. The process of etching was also suited to decorating extremely thin glassware not strong enough to take wheel-engraving. But like all processes available to him, Gallé preferred to use a variety of techniques all on the one piece, combining decoration with engraving and etching.

Although Gallé rarely used mounts on his glassware, designing them to be free standing, he liked to experiment at times with the effects gained from a bronze or silver stand with handle. The first were inspired by the Rococo and solidy conventional in their floral forms, but it was not long before his passion for naturalism saw him producing a slender sprig of silver maple leaves curling round a cameo landscape vase to form its handle, while fallen silver leaves completed the stand. Another vase showing a combination of trees and bushes had a bronze handle and mount in the form of a knobbly branch of an oak tree. More classically serpentine Art Nouveau handles of wrought iron appeared as well, but the culmination of this particular track of experiment were the silver dragonflies supporting a cameo perfume burner on the tips of their tails which in turn balanced on three lily pads. The majority of these metal mounts were produced in Gallé's workshops, but sometimes for a special commission he turned to a leading goldsmith or jeweller of the day.

Although Gallé enjoyed discovering new techniques and improving old ones, he never lost sight of the importance of subject matter. Mastery of technique was simply a means of getting closer and closer to expressing exactly what he wanted to say. The significance of his glasswork lay wholly in the chosen subject. This concern became even greater in the latter phase of his life, when his naturalism evolved into a personal form of symbolism.

OPPOSITE Enamelled glass clock from the 1890s, 7½in/19cm high.

CHAPTER FIUE
SYMBOLISM

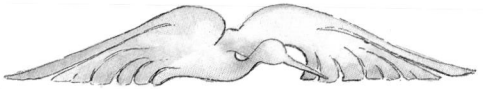

T HE FIRST GREAT OUTRAGE in Gallé's life was the invasion of his homeland by Prussian soldiers. In a trial of superpower strength, France declared war on Prussia on 19 July 1870. The French government badly miscalculated their strength. While their army was still mobilizing, the Prussians rapidly invaded France, humiliating the French in defeat after defeat. By September, the French Emperor, Napoleon III, surrendered with 83,000 French troops at Sedan, and Paris was besieged. Inside the city, the Third Republic was proclaimed and the Emperor deposed. Four months later, Paris surrendered and a peace treaty was negotiated. As the talks continued, the uprising of the Paris Commune turned the events revolutionary and there was little the French could do but accept the harsh terms dictated by Bismarck: Germany was to receive the French provinces of Alsace and most of Lorraine, and France was to pay a huge war indemnity covering the costs of their occupation.

Until this war, France had been the undisputed master of continental Europe. The trauma of defeat and the huge price they had to pay lived on in the minds of every Frenchman until 1914 when the tension exploded into war again. In 1876, work began on a national monument of commemoration and atonement, the National Vow to the Sacred Heart. This became the Basilica of the Sacré Coeur and its gleaming white domes rose above Paris on the hill of Montmartre.

Gallé served in the 23rd Line Regiment, but hardly had time to see action before the war was over and a large section of his homeland was handed over to Germany. Fortunately, Nancy remained in French territory, but only just, and this constant reminder of French defeat and Prussian conquest remained an emotional vein throughout his work, long after the conclusion of peace. In 1889, Gallé created a vase for display at the Paris Universal Exhibition – a very public statement expressing his opposition to German occupation. The subject of the vase was Joan of Arc and its inscription said: 'The peace we need is that they go back home.' Joan of Arc, represented on the vase as an embattled woman warrior on horseback, was a particularly appropriate symbol as she had been born near the province of Lorraine and visited Nancy. She was also a historical source of pride in adversity.

Gallé was intensely proud of his French heritage, taking his own name as proof of his Gallic Celtic background, and frequently quoting

ABOVE An enamelled and engraved glass vase with classical motifs, c.1890.

OPPOSITE A coupe engraved with classical motifs, shown at the Universal Exhibition of 1889.

RIGHT Butterfly vase, c.1900, made of *marqueterie de verre*.

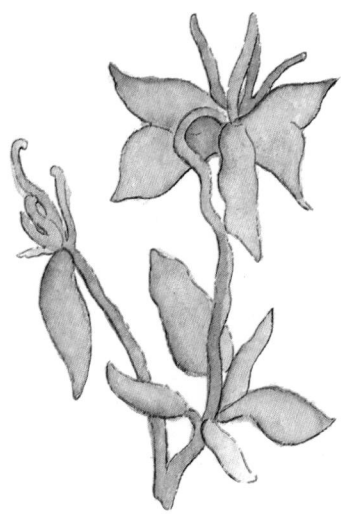

the Celtic roots of plant names to show their deep attachment to ancient man and his world of harmony with plants. The political significance of this was made obvious in his large table, *Je Tiens au Coeur de France,* also displayed at the Paris Exhibition of 1889. Intended as a public work – what he called a *table de Musée* – it was carved out of walnut and plumwood and bore a panel inside a Celtic border quoting Tacitus: *'Germania omnis a Galliis Rheno separatur'* ('The Rhine separates the Gauls from the whole of Germany'). Clearly a demand for Prussia to honour this ancient boundary and retreat from the French provinces. The grotesque figures on the legs of the table hold the shield of Lorraine while thistles, symbols of patriotism, curl in bold relief around the woodwork. Gallé signed the work *'fait par Emile Gallé de Nancy en bon espoir 1889'*. To celebrate the political alliance between France and Russia of 1893, Gallé presented a table to the Tsar of Russia on behalf of the people of Lorraine. Choosing a profusion of wild flowers to represent each town of Lorraine, he inscribed his *Flore de Lorraine* with the entreaty 'keep safe the hearts you have won' in the hope that Russia could now be relied upon to protect France against Germany. Even when Gallé chose not to feature his

ABOVE Waterlily vase, c.1900.

political views on a work, he still kept faith with his belief by inscribing the Cross of Lorraine next to his signature.

Gallé's great nationalist passion was fueled also by his love of mythology. Ever since childhood, he had been excited by tales of heroes and heroines, monsters and magic, whether they be drawn from Greek and Roman mythology or medieval Celtic cycles. These heroes were useful symbols for his own romantic inclination and he used them as emblems on his earliest work. But as he grew older, he lost interest in the explicit reference and preferred to recreate the mood of these fantastic tales, many of them seeming to express some aspect of universal psychology or some fundamental energy. He already appeared to have smothered his Christianity with a quasi-pagan worship of nature and as the years passed, he exchanged the clear botanical image of nature for a darker, less clarified evocation of mood and spirit.

One of his first major examples of this transformation from the simple image to the complicated mood is his *Orpheus and Eurydice* vase. It is the first of a series of vases in which the tragic subject is expressed symbolically by the colouring and form of the glass.

ORPHEUS AND EURYDICE

Created between 1888–89, the vase depicts the story of the doomed mythological lovers. Profoundly upset by the death of his wife Eurydice, Orpheus undertakes to descend to the Underworld where he hopes to persuade its Lord Hades to return her to him. Braving the terrible three-headed dog Cerberus at its entrance, Orpheus arrives before Hades and charms him with the beauty of his music, played upon a lyre. Hades agrees to let Eurydice return to the land of the living on the condition that he does not look back until she has reached the light. All is lost, however, when Orpheus turns back too soon, and Eurydice vanishes forever. It is a tragic tale of the inability of art to overcome the finality of death and is well suited to an artist facing his own thoughts of mortality.

For the vase, Gallé asked his good friend Victor Prouvé to design the figure of Eurydice at the moment Orpheus looks back.

His lyre has dropped to the ground and Cerberus barks mercilessly. The figures are engraved into the glass and above them is a quote from Virgil – 'Turn back no more / That would be to lose me twice / And for all time.' On this vase, the representation of the scene is not enough for Gallé: 'It has caught my fancy to work with awesome onyxes and to fold a vase in streams of lava and pitch, to incorporate the rivers Styx and Acheron on the base of the bowl, and to use a flaming meteor with the gases of hell to separate Orpheus from Eurydice who falls fainting in a sooty brown crystal.' Casting the vase with layers of black, grey and red glass, Gallé cut into these layers to create morbid clouds of swirling darkness, enhancing the setting of Hades and the mood of despairing tragedy.

Orpheus and Eurydice, 1888–89, a
carved cameo vase.

RIGHT A carved and fire-polished cameo table lamp with decorative bats on its shade, 1903, 23in/59cm high.

LEFT *L'Automne*, 1900, a blown glass vase with metallic foil inclusions and engraved, 6½in/ 17cm high.

L'Amour Chassant les Papillons Noirs shows Cupid shooting his arrow at a black butterfly against smoky grey glass, a particularly pessimistic image of love. Gallé gave the name *verres hyalites* to this glasswork, later calling them *vases de tristesse* (vases of sadness). It may be that Gallé was first intrigued by the technical achievement of creating black glass and then let it express a line of melancholy in his life. Of the glass he wrote: 'The grey glint which makes this material so iridescent comes from the reduction of iron peroxide in the coal filled air of the furnace during production.' The darkness of the glass inevitably conjured up images of night. Black, poisonous-looking flowers stood against the descending gloom of night, seemingly waiting the final touch of animal or man. Bats, wings spread round the bowl of a vase, were portrayed with huge ears, blank eyes and elongated claws, the very embodiment of vampires and creatures of the night. In *La Chauve-Souris,* Gallé combines a bat against the moon with the intoxicating poppy head, suggesting the anxious creations of dreams. The glass bears the inscription – 'Le silence des nuits panse l'âme blessée / La bonté de la nuit caresse l'âme sombre (The silence of night heals the wounded soul / The kindness of night caresses the dark soul).' Lines written by the Count Robert de Montesquiou, they are an explicit reference to the Symbolist circles to which the Count introduced Gallé.

Later, Gallé plumbed the depths of man's fear by reproducing the bottom of the sea where mysterious, forgotten creatures were believed to lurk. He portrayed this primeval environment with swaying black seaweed and ammonite-like creatures. In a vase of 1889, *Deep Sea*, a fish is translucent white with skeletal body and ragged fins. Around it, branch seaweed and an ocean bottom of black shadows are streaked with blood red. As a lover of the new science of oceanography, Gallé was fascinated by these newly discovered creatures, but it was the fact that they paralleled the fantastic dreams of man that really attracted him. He portrayed a sea-horse with its tail as the handle of a cup and gave it a fossilized texture so it could have been a prehistoric sea-dragon. Gallé's fantasies were matched by Jules Verne's *20,000 Leagues under the Sea*, published in 1870, and he must have concurred with the book's sense of wonder – 'Curious anomaly, fantastic element, in which the animal kingdom blossoms and the vegetable does not.' Seemingly to illustrate this, he created *Sea Lily* in 1895, in which the crinoid creature blooms like a flower but retains the segmented body of an invertebrate.

Searching for new symbols of sadness, Gallé took the cicada and portrayed it black against black pine needles on an amber bowl. In his mind appears to have been the Japanese idea of cicadas as harbingers of death at the peak of happiness. Spending years buried in the earth, the beetle emerges for only a few weeks of life, singing loudly and relentlessly.

ABOVE A coupe made of 'clair de lune' glass, *c.*1890, engraved.

OPPOSITE A moth-engraved vase, *c.*1902.

Flowers became part of this morbid investigation too. The *Alpine Morning Glory* 'a humble flower piercing the hard ice to enjoy an hour of sun and life' – was rendered in dark amethyst crystal with slivers of creamy snow. The *Buttercup of the Woods* is 'an intaglio study of its strangely marbled leaf, spotted with white and black, like a reptile . . . stressing the resemblance to a dragonfly, half-beast, half-plant, flying in the night, watching its prey.' And the *October Bindweed* is interpreted as the nervation of the bindweed on the base, the jade coloured stems, the grains treated like agate, the veined leaves, and even a tiny teardrop with opal relfections – the sadness of the last flower of the season.'

The morbidity of the plant world, with its seasonal cycle of death and decay, was all part of the natural history Gallé sought to understand and depict; but he could not avoid emotional involvement, choosing to express his own sad feelings through these natural symbols. In a clarifying passage from *Ecrits*, he describes his feelings of anxiety in the presence of nature: 'The poetic impression is released for those who know the beauty of the night, and who cherish the slightly disconcerting darkness of a night in the forest, the vague distress that surprises the walker in the evening, on the edge of the woods. There, in the darkness, hover strange lights, the rustle, the whispering and mysterious activity of things which are unseen, but which watch and carry on their movements in secret.'

Pursuing the effects of poetry in his glasswork through light, colour and shape, it is little wonder then that Gallé introduced lines of poetry he admired directly on to his vases. Those works that feature words most prominently are called his *verreries parlantes*, literally, talking glassware. One of the first was a brush-holder of 1884 bearing an inscription from François Villon's *La ballade des dames du temps jadis*, engraved in appropriately medieval script: *'La Reyne Blanche comme un lys, qui chantait à voix de Sirène'* ('The White Queen, like a lily who sings with the voice of a Siren'). His subsequent choice of quotations was long and exhaustive, reflecting his wide range of reading, including Virgil, Hesiod, Dante, Shakespeare, St Francis of Assisi, Gautier, Leconte de Lisle, Prudhomme, Chateaubriand, de Musset and Lamartine. The effect of these lines engraved in combination with the images they suggested is beautifully displayed in *Blue Melancholy*, a goblet of 1892. With a matt surface of cream and purple glass, Gallé introduced cloudy patches of blue which were engraved to give them the form of small petalled flowers, possibly forget-me-nots. Above the bunch of blue petals were inscribed lines by Rollinat – 'How many times a languid / Memory shows the heart / Its blue and melancholy flower.'

Gallé's favourite poets, however, were Baudelaire, Montesquiou, Victor Hugo and Maurice Maeterlinck, writers who are now described together as symbolists. Gallé was particularly impressed by an anthology of poetry by Count Robert de Montesquiou, appearing in 1892, called *Les Chauves-Souris*. Its dark atmospheric poetry inspired many of Gallé's *vases de tristesse*. They had first met in 1889 and thereafter kept up a stimulating correspondence of which Montesquiou wrote – 'A letter from Gallé is a scrawl full of wisdom, a walk taken by a

thousand *infusoa* on the sheet of paper after a preliminary bath in the inkwell. And among them are slight drawings, some sketches of cups and goblets.' Montesquiou later compared Gallé's tiny handwriting to 'an army on the march, a regiment of mites – the minute graphic symbols of the most delicate of handwritings.' It was through Montesquiou that Gallé was introduced to many of the important critics and thinkers of his day and had a view on intellectual developments in Paris.

French literature in the last quarter of the 19th century was dominated by symbolism. Baudelaire has been seen as almost providing a manifesto of this movement, calling for the affirmation of the spiritual nature of reality and the realization of the close and subtle relationship of man with the universe, as well as the concept of reality as the subjective creation of each individual's perception. In opposition to a scientific description of an object's external appearance, symbolist poets endeavoured to penetrate beneath the surface and express a deeper spiritual reality. Frequently, this deeper spiritual meaning could not be understood by logical apprehension, but only by intuitive sensitivity, evoked by allusion and suggestion. In poetry, this often led to obscurity, but the interest in mysticism and the subconscious had a clear parallel in Gallé's changing vision of nature. Intuitively, he was striving to express the inner meaning and mood of the nature around him he so admired.

Also in 1930, Gallé made a conical bowl of more particular imagery than *La Nature*, a landscape of fields and houses imprisoned behind a forest of dark tree trunks. The landscape itself is overshadowed by dense grey clouds, while the trees are leafless, straight black bars. It has the effect of a contemporary horror film in which the audience shares the viewpoint of some unidentified demon as it peers through the forest at an isolated cottage, awaiting its prey. Again, Gallé is using his craft to provoke a mood of profound, though undefined, angst.

This atmosphere of the dream, sometimes a nightmare, gained strength in his last four years after 1900. As seen, his bed, *Aube et Crépuscule,* portrayed giant moths as the bringers of dreams; in *The Hand,* a glass sculpture of a single hand reaching upwards, he is verging on the surreal. The details show the hand rising from the sea, bringing with it folded seaweed of blue and green. It is a good image of Gallé's gratitude to oceanographers for revealing the secrets of the sea, but the fact that it is not a vase or any useful celebratory object, simply a disembodied hand, a work of sculpture reaching towards nothing, gives it an unsettling air more in tune with poetry than natural history.

Les Coprins, the mushroom lamp of 1902, continues this surreal theme. Already the idea is bizarre, taking three mushrooms and turning them into shades for electric light bulbs, but given Gallé's naturalism of earlier years, in which natural form becomes the basis for design, it is not surprising. What is typical of this later period is the choice of mushrooms. They are not the attractive white-and-red spotted toadstools of our fairy-tales, but three grotesque, toxic-looking fungi. Depicted in three stages of growth, from vigorous youth to ragged capped maturity, they have emerged from the black decaying leaf mould of

OPPOSITE An engraved vase, *c.*1900.

LA NATURE

In 1900, Gallé created a bowl called simply La Nature. *It seemed to take as its inspiration a quote from Henri Martin – 'The great commune of nature'. In the glass, we see simple stains of blue and yellow, granite combinations of colour. The swirling colours, loaded with black and white grit, evoke layers of sediment, rock forms maybe, or is the blue-and-white edge of a sea lapping a seaweed-strewn beach? In the final analysis, there are so many possibilities of natural form in the piece that Gallé has succeeded in creating a vase that encompasses all aspects of the world. And like a Symbolist poem, he has achieved it through mysterious allusion – a personal collection of sensations.*

La Nature vase. From a different
angle, the bottom of the bowl
becomes a ruby red, giving the
same effect as shot silk.

La Nature vase, c.1900.

their iron base. They are an image of decay, their colours rusty browns, putrifying yellows; they are poisonous. For Gallé, the innocent charm of nature has gone, replaced by the morbid realization of death and decay. By this stage of his life, Gallé was probably aware that he was dying from leukaemia.

On 17 May 1900, Gallé was admitted to Nancy's prestigious Académie Stanislas. His acceptance speech was his most precise statement on the meaning of Symbolist decoration in his work. To begin with, he did not believe in the value of obscurity for the sake of it. 'Symbols should not be too enigmatic. The French mind likes clarity and rightly so, for, as Hugo said: 'The idea which carries the day is always clear.' Having intuitively used the flowers and plants around him for their symbolic meaning, Gallé then analyzed this assumption:

'In his Science of Beauty, *the aesthetic Levêque says that the 'weeping willow weeps no more than other willows; the violet has no more modesty than the poppy.' The moral meanings attributed to plant types are of course only symbolic . . . Here then arises a question: What decorative quality does the symbol have? Maybe the Symbolist is sacrificing the pleasure of the eyes for the games of the mind? It is certainly true that the symbol of the noblest idea still makes no greater decorative*

ABOVE Dragonfly vase, made of *verrerie parlante.*

OPPOSITE *Les Coprins* (*Ink Caps*), made 1902, blown and cased glass with a wrought-iron base, 33in/84cm high.

~ 101 ~

effect than any ordinary rose, if it is not enlivened by the accent of the design, by justification and power of the facsimile when the artist's use of colour and relief is successful. Equally it is obvious that the use of the symbol alone cannot magically confer special graces on a badly crafted, untalented decor. But who can doubt that the artist, bent over his efforts to reproduce a particular flower, insect, landscape or human face and to extract its true character, the feeling within, who can doubt that his work will be more vibrant and its emotion more contagious than that of the man with the camera and scalpel? The most scrupulously accurate naturalist's evidence, reproduced in a scientific work, cannot move us because the spiritual aspect is missing. Whereas, the reproduction of the natural Japanese artist, for example, has a unique way of translating the evocative motif or the pretty face, sometimes mocking, sometimes sad, of the living creature.

Art, therefore, is vital to the expression of the spiritual quality in nature. Having been brought up instinctively with nature, Gallé continues to support it as the ultimate source of artistic ideas:

> *Jewellers, lace-makers, they can do no more without nature than the poets. It is everyone's property, their homeground, the living source! Victor Hugo, that great agitator of symbols, admits:*
>
> > *'We could do nothing worthwhile*
> > *Without the elm and the holly.*
> > *And the birds are as much the*
> > *Authors of our poems as we.'*
>
> *Calderon pays this compliment to the flower: 'If I have found a new voice, a new heart, it is to the flower that I owe this regeneration!' And for him the flower became the symbol of reconciliation with moral beauty, with God. To banish symbols from decoration, we would have to chase our satellite from the skies, 'the golden sickle in a field of stars'. We would have to extinguish 'the evening and morning star', wipe out those apostrophes, the constellations. For the symbol to be ever more silent in art, God would have to be erased, 'the sacred star who knows our souls'. The Word in nature, for all time and across all symbols and reflections, 'That Word is God: this the constellations tell to the silence'.*

The combination of nature and God, if not in conventional religion, then certainly in some form of pantheistic belief, was all-important to Gallé. He believed that French art derived its vitality:

> *Right from the first primitive expressions, through to the moving gesture which has sent the prayer of our cathedrals soaring towards the skies. This is what made so beautiful the green expansion of the 13th century. That it was no longer shut away in a studio. Like the ivy on the oak trunk, it was climbing towards freedom, that is, towards symbolism itself. Baudelaire has a grandiose formula for the conception of creation's harmony of resonances:*
>
> > *'Nature is a temple where living pillars*
> > *Sometimes let slip confused words.*
> > *Man passes there through a forest of symbols*
> > *Which watch him with familiar glances.'*

OPPOSITE *The Hand, c.1900, decorated with applied glass shells and seaweed, 12½in/32cm high.*

OPPOSITE Two abstracted
flower design vases, using glass
marquetry.

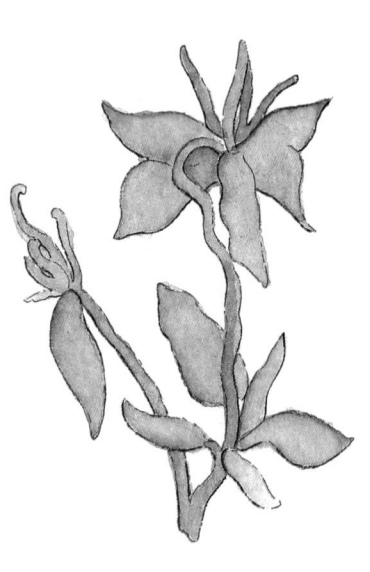

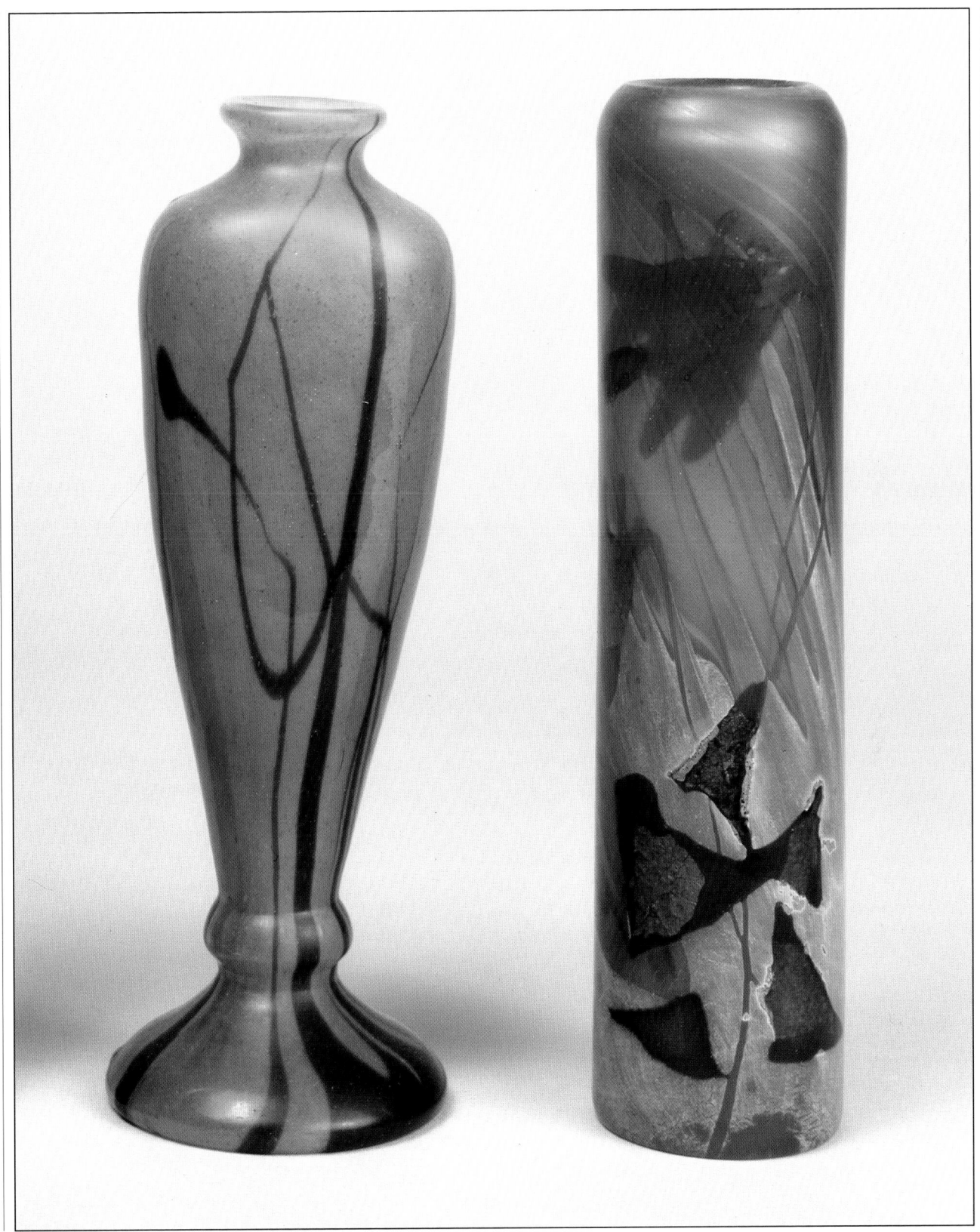

This is the story of our Celtic/Gallic national decoration, proud offspring of rude nature, scion of the druids, the bards, which always returns to its nature, to Nature, to its free spirits, to its roots, its native flora and fauna. However many invasions it suffers, from the Midi and from the East, bringing Roman fashions or those of the barbarians, nothing can destroy the joy of the artisan in the loving decoration of his home with work. Thus, popular decoration is unconsciously symbolist, like nature herself, like the holm-oak and the countryside. ... Today, our returning to the art of decoration also represents a happy return to the Brocéliande and the Celtic forests, just like those glorious national burgeonings in the 13th and 16th centuries.

It is fitting that Gallé should have chosen Bernard Palissy (1510–158) as his 16th-century example of this French tradition of naturalist art. In

many ways, Palissy reflected Gallé's own range of interests, both artistic and scientific. A French Huguenot potter who lived in Saintes, near La Rochelle, he is most famous for his dishes and bowls decorated with plants, fish and reptiles, all portrayed in full relief with every detail of their nature painted beneath the glaze. From 1575 onwards, Palissy gave lectures in Paris on natural history and scientific methods, which were later published as *Discours admirables*. He experimented with ceramics and tried to replicate the effect of Chinese porcelain. A precursor of Meissonnier and the naturalists of the Rococo, he was very much a spiritual ancestor of Gallé. It is not surprising, then, that Gallé put him in touch with an even older tradition: 'Surely it is the ancient pottery of the Gauls we see reappearing in the 'rustic amphorae' of Bernard Palissy, moulding himself carefully on nature like a fossil print, wearing real colours and glazing the objects with a liquid enamel.'

Gallé stated that in many artistic circles such craftworks are not regarded with high esteem. But he believed this natural symbolism is 'the art of the earth'. To make his point further, he quotes directly from Palissy's memoirs:

> Let us hear from the man himself what his idea was, his aim: 'A few days after the Civil War and its accompanying disturbances had died down and it had pleased our Lord to send us his peace, I was out walking through the fields around the town of Saintes, near the river Charente. Whilst I was pondering on the horrible dangers from which God had preserved me during the past tumults, I heard the voices of young girls singing the 104th Psalm. Their sweet and harmonious voices made me forget my former thoughts, and stopping to hear the psalm, I allowed the pleasure of their voices to leave me and began to contemplate the meaning itself. This is what I thought: How kind God is! My desire would be that all the works of his hands should be treated with the reverence of David in this psalm. And I thought of creating a garden to the design that the prophet describes in the psalm. The decoration and most excellent beauty would provide a refuge in the shape of an amphitheatre and a holy delight and honest occupation for mind and body.

OPPOSITE A sea anenome vase, c.1900.

Knowing God or spirituality through nature – this too is the essence of Gallé. In his defence of Palissy, Gallé concluded on a high note:

> French critics on the subject of Palissy say, 'There is no art in a pot for it has no design,' by which they mean no plan. Well, the potter at Saintes had a design, a real wish to initiate man in a vision of God by reproducing nature – through the echoes and beauties of his most humble works.

Despite Gallé's pleasure in finding a kindred soul in Palissy, he had doubts about the continuation of the natural tradition:

> Today, does the modern decorator have enough sincerity, enough faith, to make his work a source of regeneration for symbolism, of liberated art, by using a constant scrutiny of nature to achieve progress towards the highest and best ideals which have a right to be counted among an artist's preoccupations?

Gallé found hope in the discoveries and achievements of science in the 19th century, and he saw these being used to enrich the symbolic vocabulary of artists:

> Today, nature is bringing the artist new shapes. Science offers him new symbols, signs, unknown to our ancestors and yet suitable for opening eyes which have become blind to familiar things ... Even the dielytra, which was only introduced at the beginning of this century, is used today as a symbol of love and friendship with its corded form, so elegant and meaningful, its delicate flowers and the winged fold of its two outer petals ... We must admit our preference for those good old plants so dear to our forefathers. Yet modern currents are deep and rapid, too powerful for the peaceful stream of personal predilection. They carry everything before them.'

Like many artists and writers at the beginning of the new century, Gallé had a tremendous sense of faith in science and wonder at its achievement:

'On all sides, science opens to the decorator new horizons. Oceanography, of which we have a great adept among us in Nancy, is like the magic diver in A Thousand and One Nights, the king of the sea who carries away in his arms his earthly favourites so that they may visit his blue palaces.

But Gallé was not all optimism. He had strong criticism for 19th-century industrialism which destroyed the pleasure in work:

That epoch, so surprising and admirable in many ways, claimed to mass-produce decor, to flood the world with it, industrially and commercially. But it achieved that under very particular and unsatisfactory conditions. The executors of these ornaments were not able, like their ancestors, to appreciate the pure joy of the workman, in love with his craft. Even the originator trained himself to keep reproducing the past in servile copies, entirely devoid of thought. The symbols in these works were created by another age, respond to other needs, to a completely different concept of life. That is why our age cannot understand them.

For Gallé, natural symbolism was a journey of faith. 'Search honestly to know, to study and to love and they are there, for symbols will spring spontaneously in decorative art from these combined forces: the study of nature, the love of nature's art, and the need to express what one feels in one's heart.' The practise of this art was itself something religious, something transcendental: 'We must proclaim our deep faith in the doctrine which gives art a function in human culture: that of awakening spirits and souls by translating the universal beauties of the world.'

Gallé's speech to the members of the Académie Stanislas in 1900 is his single most important statement on art and its meaning to his work. In it, we appreciate all the passions that go to make up his particular view of the world: nature, God, science, and poetry.

All are quoted. All are celebrated. It is his manifesto of art and natural symbolism, his own personal contribution to the ideology of art at the time. In the conclusion to his speech, he proclaims a hope that this will form the heart of art in the future:

The term 'symbol' is often confused with the word 'art'. Consciously used or not, the symbol enlivens and qualifies the work of which it forms part: it is its soul. Now, at the dawn of the 20th century, we are able to celebrate the renewal of a national, popular art which must surely herald better times. 'It is the work of the modern artist', said Charles Albert addressing the Congress of Art in Brussels, 'which will put the stamp on the atmosphere of the coming age.' This work must be a struggle for justice within ourselves and around us. In this way, 20th-century life will not lack for joy, art or beauty.

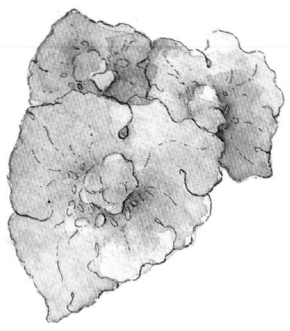

OPPOSITE *Deep Sea* vase, 1889–1903, blown and cased with applied glass and metal foil, 8in/21cm high.

THE SCHOOL OF NANCY

ABOVE Wisteria lamp, c.1900, 30½in/78cm high.

OPPOSITE Cameo table lamp, 17in/44cm high. Lamps were not a familiar form for Gallé. He began to realize their potential in the last years of his life, and the majority of his lamps were produced after his death, well into the 1920s.

IN 1901, GALLÉ FOUNDED the School of Nancy and became its president, with Antonin Daum, Louis Majorelle and Eugène Vallin as its vice-presidents. Its intention was to 'promote the rebirth and development of arts and crafts in the region', and the School soon became a leader of French Art Nouveau. But much of this had already been achieved over the previous decade, and the event simply formalized what had occurred. A school of art had grown up around Gallé as he became friends with all the leading craftsmen of the city. His influence was clear in their work, but their art also reflected the Rococo tradition and distinct naturalism of Nancy, and can only have enhanced Gallé's own ideas. If the School of Nancy was Gallé's final great achievement, it served also to reveal the remarkable assembling of talent in the city.

The brothers Antonin (1864–1930) and Auguste (1853–1909) Daum were glassmakers who embraced nature, but without the profound theorizing of Gallé. They decorated the surface of their glassware with a charm and lightness of intention that is sometimes missing in Gallé's serious statements. In the Musée des Arts Decoratifs in Paris, there is a small, transparent, conventionally shaped vase. Its grey tone sets the background for a cloudy sky. On the exterior are enamelled trees bent by a strong wind and curving round the glass bowl are engraved streaks of rain. It is a delightful scene, reminiscent of an illustration in a children's book.

Despite the difference in decorative attitude, the brothers Daum were clearly influenced by Gallé's triumph at the 1889 Universal Exhibition and set about chasing his success, showing at all the major exhibitions over the next two decades. Although they did not win the gold medals Gallé did, they nevertheless achieved a consistently high standard, sometimes shadowing Gallé's concepts. In 1900, they created the *Magnolia* and *Lotus* lamps, electric lights held in the petals of the flowers and supported on twisting, budding iron stems. A *Thistle* lamp of the same year seemed to borrow Gallé's powerful political symbolism and interpret it in the form of a glass thistle cone mounted on the spiky ironwork of Majorelle, to create a piece almost uncharacteristically strong and serious for the brothers Daum. Their cups with cicadas also seem influenced by Gallé. Like his *Beetle* vase, these portray cicadas in relief on the side of the cups; but unlike Gallé, the insects here are very much separate from the surface of the cups, not integrated

LEFT Cameo lamp, *c.*1900,
25½in/65cm high.

OPPOSITE Cameo lamps, *c.*1900.

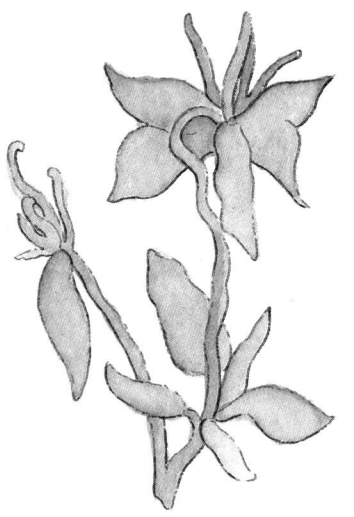

LEFT Cameo table lamp with etched dragonfly, *c.*1900.

OPPOSITE Cameo table lamps with butterfly decoration.

into a forest scene, and the subsequent effect is more surprising. A gourd-shaped vase of 1905 works best in the terms set by Gallé, being almost completely like a mottled piece of fruit with an exquisite handle, its stem, of green glass. But the brothers Daum were not philosophers of the craft as Gallé was. Their ideas did not stretch the bounds of glassware. They were happy to remain decorators and produced delightfully uncomplicated work as a result.

Louis Majorelle (1859–1929) was the leading furniture maker in Nancy. Like Gallé, he took over the business of his father and began initially to work in the 18th-century style. But by 1898, he had grasped the essence of Art Nouveau, introducing undulating, dynamic lines to chairs, tables and cabinets. He too based his designs on the forms of nature, but broke loose of the precise botanical detail that held Gallé back from creating truly liberated pieces. Gallé's limited experience of

RIGHT This ensemble of Art Nouveau furniture includes a desk by Gallé; the chair and side-table are by Majorelle, c.1900–1910.

RIGHT An acid-etched cameo
table lamp, standing 13½in/35cm
high.

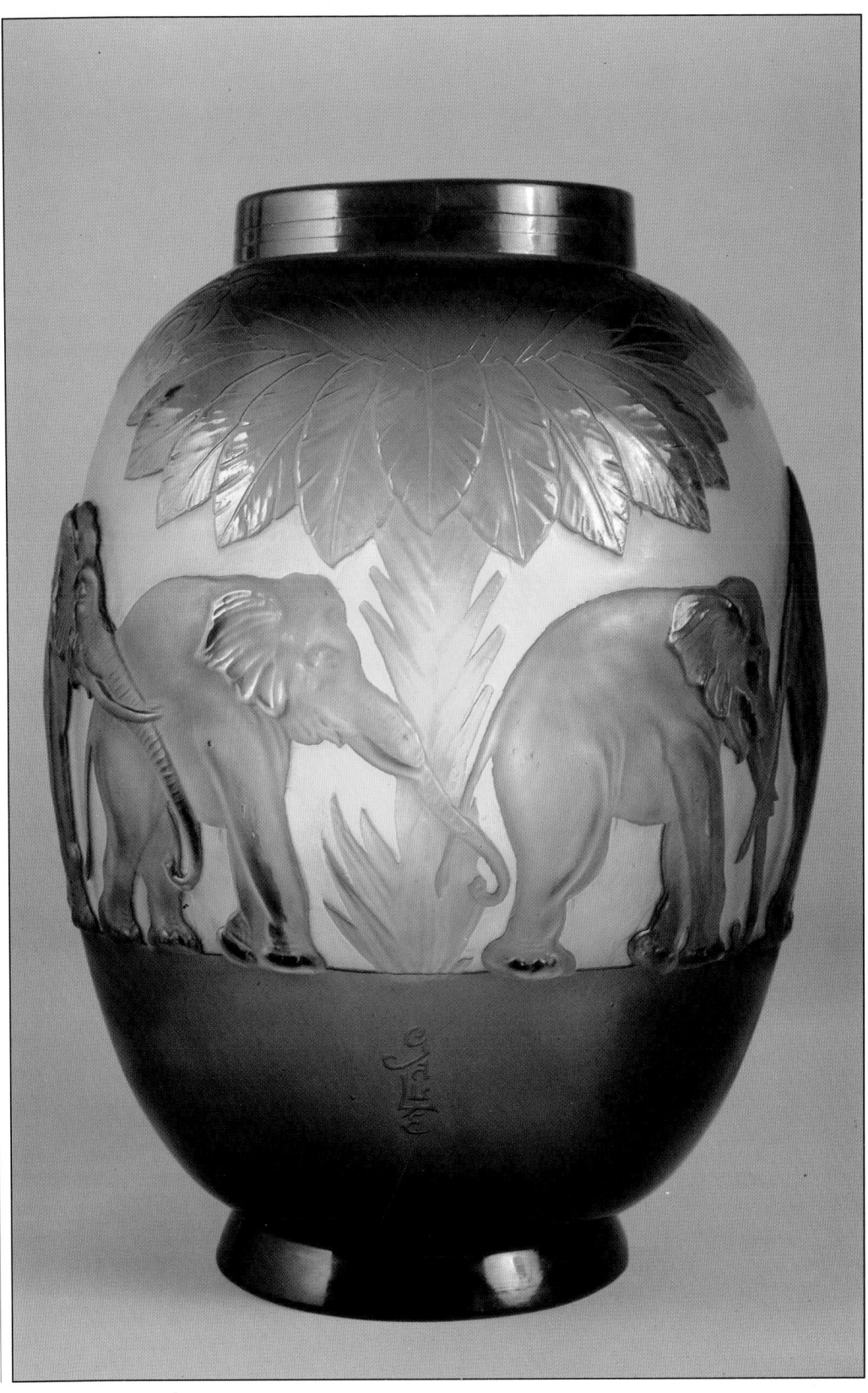

LEFT An elephant vase, mould-blown, 14½in/38cm high. This is one of a series of these lamps produced after Gallé's death for the 1925 Paris Universal Exhibition.

ABOVE A lamp with marine plant decoration, c.1910.

OPPOSITE Cameo table lamps, c.1900; the lamp on the right is in a Chinese style.

furniture design meant he was too dependent on traditional shapes for even his imagination to overcome them. Whereas in his glassware, nature inspired form, Gallé's furniture always seemed to consist of Rococo or Renaissance structures wrapped in exquisite flowers and plants – hence his reliance on marquetry to convey the luxuriance of nature detail he desired. Majorelle, however, was without the botanic obsession of Gallé and confined his plastic imagination to the flow of his furniture. Subsequently, his work was more in tune with the greater abstraction of true Art Nouveau. A supreme example of this is his ironwork for the stair-rail in Galeries Lafayette in Paris with its serpentine elegance and simple floral motifs. Eugène Vallin (1856–1922) took this development further, almost abandoning completely any floral inspiration, concentrating on strong curves anticipating the international style of Modernist art of the early 20th century.

The School of Nancy continued to set the pace for French Art Nouveau until 1904. In that year, emile Gallé died. Newspapers reported his health had been 'undermined by a mysterious illness, probably initiated by a serious haemorrhage'. In truth, it was leukaemia that killed him at the age of 58. Shortly after her husband's death, Madame Henriette Gallé sent a letter to all his clients – 'I have the honour to inform you, following the sad death of my husband, with whose works I have always been associated, that I have made the decision to retain all his employees: designers, modellers, engravers, sculptors and artisans. With the help of these devoted collaborators and thanks to the inexhaustable collection of projects and studies accumulated by Gallé himself, I will continue to produce the works of art and the techniques which have made him renowned.' Having made the decision to carry on, she then appointed their son-in-law, Paul Perdrizet, a professor at Nancy University, as the director of the family firm. Victor Prouvé remained as a close and dear family advisor.

A strong deciding factor in continuing the business was the fate of Gallé's loyal workers. They had grown to number 450, and like her husband, Madame Gallé felt a bond of responsibility to them. As a result, the industrial side of the business became uppermost, with experiments in glass sacrificed to increased efficiency of production. The vases, produced in editions of ten dozen and more, were overtly decorative, favouring the portrayal of conventional landscapes. The allusive, intrinsic natural motifs of Gallé's hand were gone, exchanged for naïve visions of a peacock sitting on a balustrade before a lake or a polar bear strutting across an icepack. This was nature as mediocre decoration. There was no one else to carry on Gallé's philosophy.

The factory continued to produce glass of an ordinary standard until 1931, when it finally shut down. Today, Gallé's workshops are gone from Nancy. Only the doors from his studio remain, solid oak carved with trees and bearing his famous motto – 'Our roots are in the depths of the woods – on the banks of streams and among the mosses.' The doors are now on display in the Musée de l'Ecole de Nancy, a museum full of many of Gallé's most important works. A fitting memorial from the city to a man and a school of art which did so much to make Nancy a centre of brilliant, internationally significant art in the last two decades of the 19th century.

Madame Gallé died in 1914, but not before she had compiled the most interesting of her late husband's writings in the *Ecrits pour l'Art* of 1908. This act has undoubtedly contributed to the fame and stature Gallé possesses in the history of glassmaking and decorative art, for it is in these essays that the depth of his enthusiasm for nature and its translation into art become clear. He was not content simply to master the craft of glassmaking and take it to new levels of colour and shape, although this alone would be enough to ensure his fame. But in his *Ecrits* there emerges an entire philosophy of art, an art with its roots firmly in a tradition of man responding to nature through creativity. He understod that man was just one part of the natural world, intimately dependent and reliant on the plants and animals around him. In the late 20th century, this message sounds clearer than ever before and should be a source of inspiration for any contemporary artist or craftsman. Not surprisingly, eloquent as ever, Gallé himself neatly summarized the essence and aim of his work: 'The study of nature, the love of nature's art, and the need to express what one feels in one's heart.'

ABOVE A cameo lamp decorated with swifts, *c.1910*.

OPPOSITE Vase with penguins, *c.1910*. This vase is typical of the unimaginative animal motifs that were so often used after Gallé's death by his factory; the integrity of form and subject that was so important to Gallé was lost after he died.

INDEX

The page numbers in *italics* refer to the captions

SELECT BIBLIOGRAPHY

Bloch-Dermant, J, *The Art of French Glass 1860–1914*, London, 1980.

Duncan, A, & Bartha, G de, *Glass by Gallé*, London, 1984.

Fourcard, L de, *Emile Gallé, Paris,* 1903.

Frantz, H, *Emile Gallé and the Decorative Artists of Nancy, The Studio,* **28**, 1903, pp. 108–117.

Fuller, P, *Theoria: Art, and the Absence of Grace*, London, 1988.

Gallé, E, *Ecrits pour l'Art,* Paris, 1908/Marseille, 1980.

Garner, P, *Gallé*, London, 1976.

Garner, P, *Glass 1900*, London, 1979.

Gros, G, *Poetry In Glass: The Art of Emile Gallé, Apollo,* 1955, pp. 134–136.

Julian, P, *The Triumph of Art Nouveau*, London, 1974.

Madsen, S T, *Sources of Art Nouveau*, Oslo, 1955.

Warmus, W, *Emile Gallé: Dreams Into Glass*, Corning Museum of Glass, New York, 1984.

ACKNOWLEDGEMENTS

Bridgeman Art Library: pages 25 (Bristol City Art Gallery), 70 (Christie, Manson & Woods, London), 96 (Private Collection), 118/9 (Private Collection). © **Christies Colour Library:** pages 11, 16/17, 30, 32, 33, 35, 37, 41, 42, 48, 54, 62/3 71, 72, 75, 76, 77, 79, 88, 91, 95, 100, 101, 105, 112, 113, 120, 121, 124, 125. **The Corning Museum of Glass:** pages 36, 38–40. **L'Institute Pasteur, Paris:** page 50. **Musée de l'Ecole de Nancy/© Studio-Image, Nancy:** pages 19, 53, 58–60, 102/3. **Musée des Arts Décoratifs, Paris/Photo L Sully Jaulmes:** 12, 15, 26, 82, 83, 87, 89, 90. **Peter Newark's Historical Pictures:** pages 6, 7, 8/9, 10. **Sotheby's, London:** 13, 18, 20–4, 27–8, 29 (courtesy Philippe Garner), 31, 34, 43–6, 49, 56, 57 (courtesy Philippe Garner), 64–5, 68–9, 73–4, 78, 80, 84, 85 (courtesy Philippe Garner), 92-3, 98–9, 106–8, 114–7, 122–3. **Victoria & Albert Museum, London:** page 66.

The author and publishers would like to acknowledge that limited quotations have been used from the following publications: W Warmus, *Emile Gallé: Dreams into Glass,* The Corning Museum of Glass, 1984; P Garner, *Gallé,* Academy Editions, 1976; P Julian, *The Triumph of Art Nouveau,* Phaidon, 1974. All other quotations are the author's own translations from original sources.